D. H. LAWRENCE

MODERN LITERATURE MONOGRAPHS

GENERAL EDITOR: Lina Mainiero

In the same series:

S. Y. AGNON   *Harold Fisch*
SHERWOOD ANDERSON   *Welford Dunaway Taylor*
LEONID ANDREYEV   *Josephine M. Newcombe*
ISAAC BABEL   *R. W. Hallett*
SIMONE DE BEAUVOIR   *Robert Cottrell*
SAUL BELLOW   *Brigitte Scheer-Schäzler*
BERTOLT BRECHT   *Willy Haas*
ALBERT CAMUS   *Carol Petersen*
WILLA CATHER   *Dorothy Tuck McFarland*
JOHN CHEEVER   *Samuel T. Coale*
COLETTE   *Robert Cottrell*
JOSEPH CONRAD   *Martin Tucker*
JULIO CORTÁZAR   *Evelyn Picon Garfield*
JOHN DOS PASSOS   *George J. Becker*
THEODORE DREISER   *James Lundquist*
FRIEDRICH DÜRRENMATT   *Armin Arnold*
T. S. ELIOT   *Joachim Seyppel*
WILLIAM FAULKNER   *Joachim Seyppel*
F. SCOTT FITZGERALD   *Rose Adrienne Gallo*
FORD MADOX FORD   *Sondra J. Stang*
JOHN FOWLES   *Barry N. Olshen*
MAX FRISCH   *Carol Petersen*
ROBERT FROST   *Elaine Barry*
GABRIEL GARCÍA MÁRQUEZ   *George R. McMurray*
MAKSIM GORKI   *Gerhard Habermann*
GÜNTER GRASS   *Kurt Lothar Tank*
ROBERT GRAVES   *Katherine Snipes*
PETER HANDKE   *Nicholas Hern*
LILLIAN HELLMAN   *Doris V. Falk*
ERNEST HEMINGWAY   *Samuel Shaw*
HERMANN HESSE   *Franz Baumer*
CHESTER HIMES   *James Lundquist*
HUGO VON HOFMANNSTHAL   *Lowell W. Bangerter*
UWE JOHNSON   *Mark Boulby*
JAMES JOYCE   *Armin Arnold*
FRANZ KAFKA   *Franz Baumer*
SINCLAIR LEWIS   *James Lundquist*
GEORG LUKÁCS   *Ehrhard Bahr and Ruth Goldschmidt Kunzer*
NORMAN MAILER   *Philip H. Bufithis*
ANDRÉ MALRAUX   *James Robert Hewitt*
THOMAS MANN   *Arnold Bauer*
CARSON MCCULLERS   *Richard M. Cook*
ALBERTO MORAVIA   *Jane E. Cottrell*
VLADIMIR NABOKOV   *Donald E. Morton*
ANAÏS NIN   *Bettina L. Knapp*

(continued on last page of book)

D. H. LAWRENCE

George J. Becker

FREDERICK UNGAR PUBLISHING CO.
NEW YORK

Copyright © 1980 by Frederick Ungar Publishing Co., Inc.
Printed in the United States of America
Design by Anita Duncan

Library of Congress Cataloging in Publication Data
Becker, George J
  D. H. Lawrence.

  (Modern literature monographs)
  Bibliography: p.
  Includes index.
  1. Lawrence, David Herbert, 1885–1930—Criticism
and interpretation.
PR6023.A93Z5664   823'.912   79-48075
ISBN 0-8044-2029-7
ISBN 0-8044-6033-7 pbk.

Lorenzo is an *experience*,
not a classic.
— *John Middleton Murry*

Contents

Chronology

1885	David Herbert Lawrence is born on September 11 in Eastwood near Nottingham, England.
1898–1901	He attends Nottingham High School on a county council scholarship.
1902–1906	He teaches school in Eastwood.
1906–1908	He takes the teacher training course at Nottingham University College.
1908–1911	He is a teacher at the Davidson Road school in Croydon.
1910	Lawrence's mother dies on December 9.
1911	*The White Peacock* is published in January.
1912	Lawrence meets Frieda von Richthofen Weekley (1879–1956) in April and goes off with her to the Continent in early May.
1913	On a summer visit to England Lawrence and Frieda meet John Middleton Murry and Katherine Mansfield. *Sons and Lovers* is published.
1914	Lawrence and Frieda are married on July 13. He receives $50 from the Royal Literary Fund.
1914–1919	Lawrence and Frieda reside in England because of the war.
1915	*The Rainbow* is suppressed in early November.
1917	The Lawrences are obliged by the police to leave Cornwall.
1919	They leave England for Italy in November.

1920–1922   The Lawrences live at the Villa Fontana Vecchia in Taormina.

1921   *Women in Love* is published. Lawrence receives the James Tait Black Memorial Prize for *The Lost Girl*.

1922   The Lawrences sail for Ceylon in February, continuing to Australia in April, and arriving in San Francisco on September 4. At the invitation of Mabel Dodge Luhan they stay in Taos, New Mexico.

1923   Lawrence makes two trips to Mexico, sailing from Vera Cruz for Europe on November 22.

1924   Lawrence returns to the United States in March, spending six months in Taos before going to Mexico in October.

1925   Lawrence is told that he has tuberculosis. He returns to Taos in April. He and Frieda return to Europe in September. They are installed at the Villa Spotorno on the Mediterranean by mid-November.

1926–1928   They reside at the Villa Mirenda, near Florence, with trips to England and Switzerland.

1928   *Lady Chatterley's Lover* is published in Florence in June.

1928–1930   The Lawrences live at various places on the French Mediterranean coast.

1929   The police raid the Warren Gallery in London on July 5 and confiscate some of Lawrence's paintings as obscene.

1930   Lawrence dies in Vence on March 2.

1935   Lawrence's body is disinterred and cremated. The ashes are brought to Kiowa ranch near Taos and placed in a small chapel.

1

•••

Fugitive and Seeker

David Herbert Lawrence (called Bert in his youth, simply Lawrence or Lorenzo in his later years) was born in the mining village of Eastwood near Nottingham on September 11, 1885. His life—with one exception—was undramatic, being merely a series of physical displacements that took him repeatedly out of England and ultimately as far afield as Ceylon, Australia, and old and New Mexico; and a series of encounters and conflicts with many of the literary figures or hangers-on of literature of his day.

Since Lawrence was only forty-five when he died of tuberculosis on March 2, 1930, virtually all his contemporaries and many of his elders outlived him. An astonishing number of them felt impelled to tell about the Lawrence they knew—in books, articles, or latterly in interviews sought by assiduous disciples of the writer. Thus we have more firsthand information about Lawrence's life than about that of any recent writer, with the possible exception of Hemingway. The gamut of delineation and evaluation is a very wide one. Unfortunately most of these accounts seek to defend or enhance the egos of the persons writing them; they therefore tend to be partisan and unreliable. At best it is possible to glean only a rough censensus—or a rough antithesis—from these many accounts.

1

There are two salient facts about Lawrence's childhood. One is the state of domestic warfare that existed between his parents, from which all five of the children suffered and from which they all sought to escape. Their father was a miner, convivial and illiterate, skilled with his hands but inarticulate. Their mother, of middle-class origin, had some knowledge of culture. The lack of amenities, the griminess of life in a mining community, the marginal economic state in which they lived made her a bitter and embattled woman, determined to achieve for her children what she had not been able to achieve for herself. Bert, in particular, was very much on his mother's side, as is evident in the basically autobiographical *Sons and Lovers*, though in later life he came to recognize that he and the others had given their father much less than his due. As Ford Madox Ford remarked: Lawrence in those days—when he made his debut in literature—"rather shudderingly" considered himself as "the product of a martyred lady-saint and a savage lower-class father."[1]

The other important fact about his childhood is that from an early age he was withdrawn from the ordinary ways of his fellows. In the recollection of his village contemporaries he was, in the local dialect, a *mardarse*, that is, a sissy. He had no boon companions until he met the Chambers family, who lived somewhat removed at Haggs Farm (the Willey Farm of *Sons and Lovers*). His happiest hours were spent in the woods and fields, where he developed an amazing knowledge and keen observation of the flora of the region. As Aldous Huxley remarked: the countryside was "at once the background and the principal personage of his novels."[2]

One of the unfortunate results of his childhood background was a nagging class consciousness. Perhaps it was inescapable in that time and place. When Lawrence was first lionized in London literary society he was automatically cast for the role of proletarian writer. People like Ford and the Asquiths wondered how to talk to a man of his origins. David Garnett thought him plebeian looking: "He was the type of the plumber's mate who goes back to fetch the tools."[3] Cecil Gray said that Lawrence "was, without qualification, the most class-conscious man I have ever known."[4] Many of his contemporaries were inclined to say sniffily that he loved a lord and that his marriage to Frieda (a baroness) and his friendship with Dorothy Brett (daughter of a viscount) were based on snobbery. The poet Rachel Annand Taylor says of Lawrence during his first London years: "He was a terrific snob, he was definitely a cad, yet in this early period he was touching, he was so artlessly trying to find his way"[5]—in decent society is the implication. Edmund Wilson goes even further: "One saw that he belonged to an inferior caste—some bred-down unripening race of the collieries. Against this inferiority—fundamental and physical—he must have had to fight all his life: his passionate spirit had made up for it by exaggerated self-assertion."[6]

Nothing in Lawrence's early years satisfactorily accounts for his range of knowledge and quickness of sensibility. Initially he was a mediocre student. Then he received a scholarship to Nottingham high school, a place where miners' sons did not go, and ultimately he made the highest score in England and Wales on a qualifying exam for the university. Early on he was discussing books and ideas with the Chambers family, he was teaching Jessie Chambers French, and he was beginning to write poetry. His intellectual growth seems, at this remove of time, to have been very nearly spontaneous. He was a genius; he was ambitious; and he was above all supremely self-confident.

With the condescension customary among Lawrence's social betters, Ford Madox Ford said of the youth's accomplishments: "I have never known any young man of his age who was so well read in all the dulnesses that spread between Milton and George Eliot. In himself alone he was the justification of the Education Act, the passage of which, a decade or so before, had split all England. He was, that is to say, the miner's son with nothing but pennies to spend on his education . . . and he moved amongst the high things of culture with a tranquil assurance that no one trained like myself in the famous middle-class schools of the country ever exhibited or desired."[7]

One other aspect of Lawrence's formative years demands attention—his sexual experience. The archapostle of sexual liberation feared sex. It is likely that his initiation came late, when he was well into his twenties. Catherine Carswell detected in him a working-class prudishness; he was not an advocate of the nude but believed in "natural reticence."[8] He had to work to throw off the taboos of his milieu and his education. At college, for example, an English teacher told him that "stallion" was "a word we do not use." Lawrence took this to heart: there are a good many stallions, boldly named, in his fiction. Witter Bynner, who knew him in Mexico and New Mexico, called him "a sort of Freudian prig."[9] John Middleton Murry, a close friend off and on during the war years, commented that Lawrence had "a curiously intense preoccupation with 'the animal of himself,' which fascinated and repelled him. Lawrence, it should never be forgotten, was a Puritan and something of a Manichee."[10]

There can be no question that his attachment to

and domination by his mother did him serious damage. He confessed on more than one occasion that his attitude toward her was that of a lover. As a young man he seems both to have desired and feared involvement with a woman on a sexual level. This conflict was quickly resolved when he met Frieda Weekley, who was married and six years older than he, and whom many of his acquaintances described as a kind of Earth Goddess or Earth Mother.

Even so, marriage did not completely allay his anxiety. Cecil Gray observed that a man who has complete and satisfying sexual experience "is never obsessed with sex to the extent to which Lawrence was in his writings ... it is the Swinburnes and Nietzsches and Lawrences who persistently glorify and magnify the joys they have never really experienced in all their fullness, if at all."[11] It is his unsubstantiated judgment that Lawrence was very near to impotence. Murry came to something of the same conclusion: "I felt that his demand for a more intimate relation with me sprang from the fact that some element in his nature was left profoundly unsatisfied by his marriage."

A number of his contemporaries looked upon Lawrence as a latent homosexual. Orioli, his Florentine publisher, wrote flatly: "Lawrence was a homosexual gone wrong; repressed in childhood by a puritan environment. That is the key to his life and his writings."[12] Cecil Gray again, who had read Lawrence's tract "Goats and Compasses" (later destroyed by the author), calls that work "a bombastic, pseudo-mystical, psycho-philosophical treatise dealing largely with homosexuality—a subject, by the way, in which Lawrence displayed a suspiciously lively interest at that time" (around 1916).[13] In a discarded preface to *Women in Love* Lawrence states that at age sixteen he had a sexual encounter with a young miner that was the most intense experience of his life. This may account for his feeling of incompleteness in heterosexual relations, his unavailing search for a male friend to give him a sense of complete being, and the fact that his male acquaintances generally turned against him, or he against them, after a time. However, it must be emphasized that there is no evidence of sexual activity outside of wedlock. At most a revulsion against whatever secret desires he may have had was at war with a theoretical belief in sexual fulfillment in whatever way one's nature demanded. We simply do not know, and cannot know, enough about Lawrence's psyche to do more than speculate about the sources of his art and the fantasies it may have embodied.

It was in 1911 and 1912 that Lawrence, the provincial genius from an obscure mining village, a schoolteacher who hated his vocation, succeeded in breaking with his past. His mother's death in December 1910 was a great, though liberating, blow. He struggled disconsolately through the next few months. Then in November he had a bout of pneumonia so severe that he gave up his teaching post at Croydon and determined to begin a new life. It was in April 1912 that the great dramatic event of his life took place. Calling on a Professor Ernest Weekley to inquire about a possible teaching post in Germany, he met Weekley's German wife, Frieda. It was as though lightning had struck both of them. In a matter of weeks Frieda had decided to leave her three children and go off to the Continent with Lawrence. He had only eleven pounds in his pocket, she not much more. From that point on they lived, often precariously, from the proceeds of his writing.

This was the turning point in Lawrence's life. Without Frieda it is doubtful that he would have achieved the power and depth that characterize his mature work. Indeed, it is doubtful that his tortured psyche would have held together sufficiently for him to have continued to write at all. Even though their relationship was tempestuous, with outbursts of almost uncontrolled violence on Lawrence's part and with deep-seated maternal guilt on the part of Frieda, their life together did last. The couple did come through. Frieda brought her lover three inestimable gifts: a healthy and uninhibited attitude toward sex, patience and compassion that weathered all storms, and an unshakable conviction as to Lawrence's potential as a writer.

Frieda was an effective antidote to Lawrence's inhibiting and emotionally sterile upbringing and his experience with Jessie Chambers. The German woman was lusty and down to earth, vitally human, secure in her belief that sex was a gift to be enjoyed. Late in life, John Middleton Murry, who had been her lover for a time after Lawrence's death, wrote that she had given him "something that I needed terribly: as it were opened a new world to me."[14] This must have been even more true for Lawrence, whom she consciously and strenuously attempted to bring to a new and vital embrace of life. It gave her great satisfaction to defeat Jessie Chambers. As Frieda wrote to Harry T. Moore, the only way to counter the "superiority" of women like Jessie was to "bash it with a hatchet." "I detest her in her arrogance and 'virginity,' they try to come it over men that way, but this time it did not work!"[15] The sudden passional depth and growth of understanding of sexual needs and motives evident in *Sons and Lovers* and its successors must be attributed to Frieda.

Equally important was her compassion. As she wrote Murry, "from a rational, accepted social conventional point of view" Lawrence was impossible. "But then at bottom I always felt that there was an inevitable thing there and he had to live by his own laws and I did not bear him any grudge," although she admits she was unhappy at times.[16] In another letter to Murry she recalls: "I felt so terribly sorry for him or I never could have stood it all." On occasion she was frightened when Lawrence "went over the edge of sanity," recalling an incident when he almost choked her to death, grinding out the words: "I am the master, I am the master."[17] She wishes she had handled him better, "but how can a poor woman handle a thunderstorm?" At any rate, handle him she did to the best of her ability. No one could have done it better.

Finally, there was her sense of mission, to make Lawrence, or to allow him to become, the great writer that she was convinced he was potentially. In 1951 whe wrote Edward Gilbert—to her mind a prying and imperceptive academic—that she was the first person to see Lawrence's significance: "It is my riches, my glory, my deepest conviction that I was part of his work as I was of his life and a vital part . . ."[18] She long resented the condescension she met among his literary friends. As she wrote F. R. Leavis, whose judgments she disliked, she may not have been an intellectual, "but I wasn't dumb either . . ."[19] To be sure, these statements are somewhat self-serving, since to have nurtured Lawrence's genius and his fame was to justify her own life.

After a few months spent with Frieda's relatives in Germany the couple set off on foot for Italy; in their knapsacks they carried their few possessions, including a spirit lamp on which to cook along the way. They spent the winter in Italy, went back to England for two months in the summer of 1913, spent the fall and winter in Italy again, and in June 1914 returned to England, Frieda by way of Germany, Lawrence walking across Switzerland to France through the St. Bernard Pass. They were married in July. Then, caught by the war, they lived a desperate and harried existence for more than five years in spartan lodgings or in cottages lent by friends until they were finally able to leave for Italy once more in November 1919. Thereafter their life was spent abroad with only brief returns to England and Germany.

As for all the idealists of that generation, World War I came as a bitter blow to Lawrence. It was a collective insanity that reinforced his misanthropy and at once sharpened and undermined his hopes for an ideal human state. If Bertrand Russell is right that "he lived in a solitary world of his own imaginings,"[20] the general and personal experience of the war brought Lawrence harshly back to reality. He was periodically subjected to physical examination to determine his fitness for military service. This he considered debasing and humiliating. He and Frieda were forced to leave their retreat on the Cornish coast in October 1917 because of anti-German feeling and a rumor that the couple were spying for the enemy. They were penniless. A friend and neighbor provided the money for them to get to London. Earlier in the year, when Lawrence wanted to go to the United States, he was denied a passport. Frieda said that something changed forever in Lawrence as a result of this expulsion, but it is more likely that the wartime experience merely aggravated an already existent feeling that England was a prison. Unlike the other revelers on Armistice Day 1918, Lawrence was pessimistic. He was con-

vinced that the Germans would rise again, and that
hatred rather than peace would continue to prevail
on earth. Richard Aldington commented about
Lawrence just before his departure from England
late in 1919: "There was no place for him in that
rather sinister post-war world. Either he must escape from it or it would crush him. He had to go into
the wilderness or perish, cease to be the unique
thing he was."[21]

Escape he did, and for the remaining eleven
years of his life he and Frieda restlessly wandered
the earth without finding the harborage they
sought. Lawrence was constantly ambivalent about
England. When he was out of England, he longed
for it; when he was there, he was impatient to flee
again. Almost the first words Lawrence uttered
when he came back from New Mexico in the winter
of 1923 were: "I can't bear it." He felt like a wild
beast in a cage. In any case, he never stayed long in
England. Capri and Taormina provided a refuge in
1920 and 1921. In early 1922, in hesitant acceptance
of Mabel Dodge Sterne's invitation to come to her
in New Mexico, Lawrence and Frieda sailed for
Ceylon, where he found what he had already antici-
pated, that Eastern mysticism was not for him. At
last, after a few months in Australia, the Lawrences
sailed for San Francisco, where they arrived on September 5, 1922. In Taos, in spite of resentment over
the patronage of Mabel Sterne, Lawrence found a
considerable degree of peace and well-being. As he
wrote: "I think New Mexico was the greatest experience from the outside world that I ever had . . .
New Mexico . . . liberated me from the present era
of civilization, the great era of material and mechanical development."

During the next two years there were two so-
journs in Mexico, where, characteristically, he was

both drawn to and repelled by the primitive alien culture. In February 1925, already suffering from malaria, Lawrence was diagnosed as having tuberculosis in the third degree and was given a year or two to live. He returned to New Mexico for the warm season, but the prospect of a winter there was frightening and he sailed for Europe in late September 1925, never to return.

It is almost beyond belief that after this diagnosis Lawrence made no effort to get medical treatment. His condition was of long standing: as early as 1913 David Garnett witnessed a hemorrhage. In the later years he hemorrhaged periodically and suffered a generally lowered vitality. There was a bad bleeding in the summer of 1927 from which it took him six weeks to recover. In January 1928 he went to Switzerland, where for a time he felt better. He kept moving about, always expecting improvement, but without medical attention, and engaging in activities that taxed his waning strength. He did consult a doctor in Germany in the fall of 1929, and at Bandol near Marseilles he was under the care of Dr. Andrew Morland, who dated his condition from the poverty-stricken war years in England. On February 6, 1930, he was so much worse that he moved to a nursing home in Vence, where he was visited by H. G. Wells and the Aga Khan, as well as the Aldous Huxleys. The sculptor Jo Davidson made a head of him there. Lawrence became restless in the sanitorium, and a few days before his death he was moved to a house in Vence, where he died on March 2, 1930. There was a simple funeral at which Frieda said "Goodbye, Lorenzo." Later his body was cremated and the ashes removed to Frieda's ranch in New Mexico, where the grave has become a shrine much sought by literary pilgrims.

The years after the return from New Mexico

were not particularly productive ones—except for
Lady Chatterley's Lover. They were years of maxi-
mum frustration because of the action taken by British and American authorities against his works as
obscene. He was aware that there would be trouble
because of *Lady Chatterley* and had an edition of
1000 copies printed privately in Florence for sale
by subscription. (Up to July 10, 1929, the profits
from this venture were £1615.) Copies were inter-
cepted by postal authorities on both sides of the Atlantic. Then there was the interception of two in-
complete manuscripts of *Pansies* in 1929: Lawrence
quite rightly thought that the British post office
looked askance at anything mailed from Bandol. Finally there was the furore caused by the exhibition
of his paintings at the Warren Gallery in London in
June–July 1929. Eight paintings and five watercolors were seized by the police (under the Obscen-
ities Act of 1857, which actually applied only to "the
suppression of trade in obscene articles"). For a
time it was feared that the paintings would be
burned, but after negotiation they were saved.
These acts of censorship and seizure made Lawrence one of the best-known English writers at his
death, but it was a notoriety that obscured his real
talent and his real significance, and made necessary
the rather tiresome apologies of his disciples and
defenders.

That significance has two aspects. For the short
term there was his influence on others. He was in
his way charismatic. For those who were willing to
accept Lawrence on his own terms, communion
with him was an exhilarating, indeed a liberating,
experience. His quick sympathy for flowers, animals, and simple people—in short, those that did
not make excessive demands of him—was a revelation of hidden potentialities for living. His Ameri-

can publisher, Thomas Seltzer, who spent New Year's at the Lawrence ranch in 1923, said "he was as great a man as he was a writer. In every aspect of life he was natural, without pose and, at bottom, sane."[22] Harriet Monroe, the poet, who met him briefly in Chicago, responded immediately to the "urge for life" that one felt in his company.[23] Catherine Carswell, a Scottish novelist, who became a lifelong friend, records that in conversation "he gave an immediate sense of freedom, and his responses were so perfectly fresh, while they were puzzling, that it seemed a waste of time to talk about anything with him except one's real concerns."[24] Lady Cynthia Asquith, from a quite different social milieu, attested to "his difference from other people. It was not a difference of degree; it was a difference of kind. Some electric, elemental quality gave him a flickering radiance. Apart from this strange otherness, one could see that he was preternaturally alive."[25]

In spite of childhood conditioning against the man who ran off with their mother, all three of the Weekley children found him attractive. The response of Montague Weekley, who did not meet him until 1926, is particularly indicative: "The blue eyes in Lawrence's bearded face seemed to be alight with an almost disturbing vitality, as though our meeting had re-kindled all the intensity smouldering within him."[26] Rhys Davies, a Welsh writer, attests of Lawrence a year before his death: He was "a Christ of himself as every man can become who has once found the pure centre of his being and keeps it uncontaminated . . . Civilization had not dirtied him, in himself, though enough mud was thrown at him, and some clung for a space."[27] Finally, Aldous Huxley, a good and compassionate friend in spite of his satiric portrait of Lawrence in

Point Counterpoint, gave this judgment: "What mattered was always Lawrence himself, was the fire that burned within him, that glowed with so strange and marvellous a radiance in almost all he wrote."[28]

Of course, there were also those whose assessments were reserved or downright hostile. They were the ones who observed that conversation with Lawrence was a one-way street, that he did not brook disagreement. Philip Heseltine (who wrote under the pseudonym of Peter Warlock) turned against him completely, asserting that "personal relationship with him is impossible—he acts as a subtle and deadly poison."[29] Witter Bynner, always a somewhat hostile witness, concluded after traveling with Lawrence in Mexico that he was "utterly without imagination, humor, or warmth—the qualities of any first-rate creator . . . I am convinced that it is himself that he despises and makes mankind vicariously suffer for."[30] A more tolerant view comes from the writer, Eleanor Farjeon, who, acknowledging "his uncontrolled irritabilities," concedes "that a volcano is not really responsible for its own eruptions."[31] It is proper to give Frieda the last word on his unevenness of temper: "Healthy in soul he always was. He may have been cross and irritable sometimes but he was never sorry for himself and all he suffered."[32]

In the long run, of course, it is Lawrence's writings that determine his enduring significance. In the twenty years of his active authorship he produced works of remarkable range. Trusting in his intuition, he did not hesitate to step forth into areas where a more cautious man might have feared to tread. He produced two volumes on the psychology of the unconscious, four volumes of travel impressions, one of which is a minor classic, a highly individual book on classical American literature, eight plays, and enough verse to qualify him as a major poet—all this in addition to his major activity as a novelist and writer of short fiction. And we must add that after his return from New Mexico in 1925 he seriously took up painting and showed a powerful originality in that medium.

Lawrence began and ended his career as a poet. In all, he published ten volumes of verse during his lifetime. After his death Richard Aldington and Giuseppe Orioli brought out a volume called *Last Poems* (1932) that contains some of his most moving verse. His poems may be divided into five groupings: the verse written before he went off with Frieda, which is groping and eclectic, and largely derivative; the confessional poems of *Look! We Have Come Through!* (1917), which reveal the emotional stresses of marriage and which Aldous Huxley characterized as embarrassing as opening the wrong bedroom door at a house party; the collection, *Birds, Beasts* and *Flowers* (1923), which deserts human emotion; the collections of *Pansies* (1929), *Nettles* (1930), and "More Pansies" (1932), which are satiric, misanthropic, and frequently banal; and finally a few very poignant poems written in contemplation of death.

Critics (and readers, for that matter) are sharply and irreconcilably divided in their judgment of Lawrence's poetry. The Lorenzophiles, of course, consider everything from his pen to be important, if not as art, then as revelation of a unique personality. That is fair enough, though it does demand attention for a considerable body of bad poetry. The real issue is the difference of opinion between those critics who believe that technically Lawrence broke new ground with his essentially free-verse form, and those who see his poems as undisciplined outpourings, sparks struck by the poet's uncertain tem-

per in contact with the world, reactive as he vents
his anguish or his spleen, but without the compression or distillation of art.

There is no question that Lawrence had a very
definite idea as to what he was doing once his derivative period was over. In his preface to the American edition of *New Poems* (1918), he challenges the
ideas of most writers of free verse, who merely
"break the lovely form of metrical verse" and "dish
up the fragments as a new substance." "They do not
know that free verse has its own *nature,* that it is
neither star nor pearl, but instantaneous like plasm.
It has no goal in either eternity. It has no finish. It
has no satisfying stability, satisfying to those who
like the immutable. None of this. It is the instant;
the quick; the very jetting source of all will-be and
has-been. The utterance is like a spasm, naked contact with all influences at once. It does not want to
get anywhere. It just takes place. For such utterance
any externally-applied law would be mere shackles
and death. The law must come each time from
within."

If we are to find in this statement anything
more than a confession of incapacity, or unwilling-
ness, to accept discipline, we need an interpreter.
Sandra M. Gilbert, who has examined Lawrence's
poetry in *Acts of Attention* (1972), believes that a
poem is a perceptual experience that both poet and
reader must undergo. The poem constitutes a
process of discovery, and that "experience of discovery is as much the subject of the poem as the
ostensible subject itself."[33] On these grounds the casual, improvised, unfinished nature of the poems is
legitimate, part of the dialectic of discovery in
which reader is pitted against poetic speaker or, on
occasion, merely listens as poetic speaker number
one struggles with poetic speaker number two to

winnow out the truth. The effort is to submerge the reader-observer in the object and let his "intuitional blood consciousness" take over. Poetry, then, is less a finished and appealing aesthetic object than it is an epistemological method.[34]

A rather surprising defender of Lawrence's poetry is W. H. Auden (in *The Dyer's Hand*, 1963). He admits that it was Lawrence's message that first made an impression on him and that the poetry "offended my notions of what poetry should be."[35] Auden says his views of poetry haven't changed but that there are Lawrence poems that he admires enormously, especially in the *Birds, Beasts and Flowers* volume, where the poet is "intensively concerned with a single subject, a bat, a tortoise, a fig tree, which he broods on until he has exhausted its possibilities."[36] Auden accepts the format of the poems, pointing out that it took Lawrence a long time to find a means of expression of sufficient originality to cope with the originality of his sensibility. He comments that Walt Whitman has not had a beneficial influence on any English poet except Lawrence. Auden thinks that Lawrence is often turgid and obscure when discussing people or ideas, but that when "he is contemplating some object with love, the lucidity of his language matches the intensity of his vision."[37]

This is all very well, but the majority of readers find the poetry difficult and generally unrewarding. The poems are tentative and repetitious. They usually go on too long. They do not arrive at a conclusion. Once in a while out of the chrysalis of process there does burst a perfect poem. Then the method seems justified, but these fairly rare achievements intensify one's irritation that the poet did not more often reach such perfection and that he was too willing to offer up working papers, first drafts, *ébauches* as completed poems. It is unfair, considering his theories, to single out certain poems as the high point of his writing, and of course such a choice risks being the kiss of death in the way that inclusion in an anthology threatens fossilization of a living work. However, from *Look! We Have Come Through!*, "Bei Hennef," "Gloire de Dijon," "Frohnleichnam," and "Song of a Man Who Is Loved" stand out as distillations of emotion going beyond mere notation. Among later poems, "TheElephant Is Slow to Mate" has a perfection that makes one think of Auden at his sardonic best. In the poems written in anticipation of death, the wonderfully moving "Bavarian Gentians" and "The Ship of Death" are a crowning achievement.

Of Lawrence's eight plays there is little to say in commendation. The drama was definitely not his forte. Most of these works are early, five of them drawing on his youthful experience in Eastwood. Most of them, also, are merely projections to the stage of bits of his own experience, or extrapolations from it. *The Widowing of Mrs. Holroyd* (1914), the only one that approaches dramatic power, is a rendering for the stage of the situation in the short story, "Odour of Chrysanthemums," based on the conflict between Lawrence's parents. At the point where the mother decides to leave her husband, an unconsciously wished for resolution occurs with the death of the miner husband. Here the play transcends mere transcription and takes on universal tones of grief. *The Daughter-in-Law* portrays a possessive mother. *A Collier's Friday Night* (1909) is a genre piece once more exhibiting domestic dissension, drawing also on the writer's school experiences and his relations with Jessie Chambers. *Touch and Go* (1920) is an offshoot of the novel *Women in Love*. It portrays a miners' strike, with

Gerald Crich as one of the protagonists. In *Fight for Barbara* Lawrence dramatizes in his imagination the efforts of an eloping wife's parents to make her return to her responsibilities. This was written a few months after Lawrence's departure with Frieda. Two of the plays, *The Married Man* and *The Merry-Go-Round*, are attempts at conventional comedy. Neither play gets off the ground. Plot and language are stiff, the situations mechanical. These novice exercises are best forgotten. Their chief virtue is the authentic use of dialect, for which Lawrence had a keen ear.

Two of the plays were actually produced. *The Widowing of Mrs. Holroyd* was put on by an amateur group at Altrincham (near Chester) in February 1920, and again in London in December 1926. *Touch and Go* was refused by the People's Theatre Society as impossible to produce. Lawrence's late play *David,* a poetic drama written in 1925, embodying his favorite theme of blood brotherhood, was also produced in London in May 1927. Its reception was unfavorable. The author blamed "those mangy feeble reviewers."[38]

Of the four volumes of travel impressions that Lawrence wrote, *Sea and Sardinia* (1921) is a classic. The others, *Twilight in Italy* (1916), *Mornings in Mexico* (1927), and *Etruscan Places* (1932), are less unified but still have the peculiar intensity of observation that characterizes their author. No matter that these works are really potboilers, tossed off rapidly to make money. They all have a vividness and an eye for revealing detail that have given them a permanent readership.

Lawrence's intuitive feeling for landscape and people is what sets these works apart from the common run of travel impressions. *Sea and Sardinia,* an account of a short trip he and Frieda made in Janu-

ary–February 1921, was written entirely from
memory immediately on their return to Taormina.
Unpretentious and minimally tendentious, it revels
in the primitiveness of isolated Sardinia (a half century before the touristic exploitation of the Aga
Khan). *Twilight in Italy* puts together impressions
gathered on the walking trip from Germany to Italy
that he and Frieda made in the first year of their
union, and adds accounts of later excursions to out-
of-the-way parts of Italy. *Etruscan Places* is based
on a trip Lawrence made with his friend Earl H.
Brewster to the Etruscan tombs northwest of Rome.
It plays off the debased present against an idealized
past of the Etruscans, in whom Lawrence found an
idyllic, prelapsarian spontaneity of living. It does
not matter that their language cannot be read and
that their way of life is a matter of wild surmise.
Lawrence endowed them with an integrity of being
that was his ideal and saw in them a life-giving community of spirit or, as he customarily put it, of the
blood. *Mornings in Mexico,* which in fact contains
some sketches of New Mexico, is a kind of pendant
to the Mexican novel, *The Plumed Serpent.* Again
Lawrence sees what he wants to see beneath the
physical and social landscape. Mexico is cruel, dark,
and foreboding. The Indian primitive is unassimila-
ble to the ways of the conqueror, be he Spaniard or
Yanqui.

It is to be noted that in his travels Lawrence
always sought the unspoiled primitive and that he
was generally disappointed. It must also be remarked that his encounters with the primitive were
generally brief and superficial, which did not deter
him from making emphatic intuitive judgments.
However reluctantly, he did have to surrender his
dream of a healthy primitive state to which he and
his like-minded contemporaries could return in fa-

vor of the much more difficult feat of sloughing off one's old consciousness in favor of a new one.

This conception is central to his principal effort at literary criticism, *Studies in Classic American Literature* (1923). Here it is not the physical landscape of America, which he knew only casually (and at a later date), but the moral landscape of its literature in the eighteenth and nineteenth centuries from which he drew his conclusions. The volume is really not literary criticism but an examination of an odd series of writers to make a Lawrentian doctrinal point. As we might expect, he chooses only those works that will support his preconceptions and does considerable violence to them in support of his predetermined conclusion.

As Lawrence sees the American experience, it is reflected in a dual rhythm of art-activity. There is a disintegration and sloughing off of the old European consciousness and the forming of a new consciousness underneath.[39] On the surface American romance is "as nice as pie, goody-goody and lovey-dovey." But underneath, it is devilish, dominated by a need to destroy "the whole corpus of the white psyche, the white consciousness," and to do it secretly.[40] Lawrence berates the American addiction to transcendentalism, to the ideal, with the result that this country has never been "a blood-home-land, only an ideal home-land."[41] And idealism leads to death. It is in the discussion of *Moby Dick* that he pushes this thesis to the limit. The white whale is "the deepest blood-being of the white race," which is "hunted by the maniacal fanaticism of our white mental consciousness, which saps and destroys blood-consciousness."[42]

In Walt Whitman, whom he admires greatly, Lawrence finds the heroic message that the soul is not to pile up defenses around itself or to seek its heaven inwardly in mystical ecstasies. It must go down the open road, experiencing in company with those other experiencing souls whom it encounters. Whitman does, however, make the mistake of confounding comradely sympathy with Jesus' love and St. Paul's charity, which lead to death, not life.[43]

The virtue of this iconoclastic work is that it brought into question the conventional images of America's good grey writers, tore off their aura of sanctity, and probed for the covert rather than the ostensible or official meaning. However, Lawrence chose his texts capriciously, mining where he found suitable ore and neglecting authors and works that did not support his argument. His style in this work, which initially seems pleasantly nonacademic, palls by the repetition of flippancy. There is a great deal of self-reference as the argument proceeds. The book is provocative, but more illuminating of Lawrence than of its subject.

Indeed, Lawrence did not seek to be a literary critic in a formal sense. He wrote a long manuscript on Thomas Hardy, which is more about Lawrence than about Hardy's writing. Through the years there was a running and hostile commentary on Dostoevsky, which had little to do with Dostoevsky the novelist, and which served besides to irritate Middleton Murry. His best criticism is to be found in the introductions to the stories by Giovanni Verga, the Sicilian realist, many of whose works he translated.

There was one more artistic venture. Lawrence started painting seriously at the Villa Scandicci in the fall of 1926, using canvases that Maria Huxley had left there. Each of the paintings he produced was a great satisfaction to him, not only because of the pleasure of a new medium but because in those combative years of writing and publishing *Lady*

Chatterley's Lover he saw the pictures as a further challenge to middle-class stuffiness. As early as the end of February 1927 he was writing to Earl Brewster that he puts a phallus in each of his pictures somewhere. "And I paint no picture that won't shock people's castrated social spirituality. I do this out of positive belief, that the phallus is a great sacred image: it represents a deep, deep life which has been denied in us, and still is denied."[44]

In line with this challenge most of Lawrence's paintings are of nudes and recall Renoir's exuberance of flesh. To mention only a few, *Rape of the Sabine Women* is a swirl of naked flesh, mostly buttocks. *Boccaccio Story* shows a group of habited nuns converging on a naked, sleeping gardener. *Family on a Veranda* represents a complacent bourgeois family nakedly taking their ease on a veranda. *Contadini* represents a single peasant, his naked torso cut off just *below* the penis. This last painting has great strength; others are ingratiating by their fluidity of line. Some, like *Throwing Back the Apple*, a protest demonstration by Eve, are witty.

Unfortunately the exhibition planned at the Warren Gallery in London for October 1928 had to be deferred. By the time it did open on June 16, 1929, the hue and cry over *Lady Chatterley's Lover* was at a high pitch. Thus press notices of the exhibition were almost universally condemnatory. That of Paul Konody in *The Observer* is a good example: "This author-artist, weary, perhaps, of being subtly misbehaved in print, has elected to come straight to the point, and is frankly disgusting in paint."[45] Naturally such notices only served as an advertisement. People flocked to the exhibition. Then on July 5, the day after a gala evening attended by Frieda Lawrence, the police raided the gallery, impounding eight of the sixteen paintings and five of the nine watercolors on view. They also impounded, temporarily, a copy of William Blake's *Pencil Drawings* under the impression that he was a contemporary. What was left of the exhibition continued for another seven weeks, the vacant places on the wall being filled with watercolors done by Lawrence many years before. Undoubtedly the raid and the generally adverse reviews were occasion for outrage on Lawrence's part, but he did succeed in his avowed intention of making so-called official morality ridiculous.

Whatever his interest in other artistic forms, Lawrence was preeminently a writer of prose fiction. It is on his ten novels and his sixty-odd pieces of shorter prose fiction that his reputation rests. To determine Lawrence's continuing importance, the best thing we can do is to examine his prose works in as much detail as a volume of this scope will permit.

2

●●

Sons and Lovers

It is customary to speak of *Sons and Lovers* as an autobiographical novel since its materials are drawn from and are parallel to those of Lawrence's early life. The Morel family is to all intents and purposes the Lawrence family. Bestwood is Eastwood. Willey Farm and the Leivers family are Haggs Farm and the Chambers. Above all Miriam Leivers is Jessie Chambers, the girl to whom Lawrence was close for more than ten years.

However, it is a mistake to expect a point to point correspondence of novel and life or to attempt to clarify details of the writer's life by drawing from the novel. What has happened here, as usually happens in the best autobiographical novels, is that the writer moves from the particular—his own life—to the general, an account exemplary of some aspect of the human condition. He thus makes his fiction generic or universal. The details of the life are the matrix—or, better, the springboard—for a subtly rearranged and amplified statement that may, in extreme cases, actually contradict the life in major ways.

This is fortunate for us, and indeed for Lawrence's continuing fame. After seventy years we have a diminishing interest in the shaping forces and sexual frustrations of the writer's youth, but we are readily drawn into the life of Paul Morel, whose fictive experiences correspond with those of a substantial number of young men in any generation. This exemplary quality of the work is further reinforced by historical accident. In advance of ever hearing or reading about Freud's Oedipus complex, Lawrence in his novel produced a classic study of that situation, causing Alice Meynell and Ivy Low eagerly to proclaim *Sons and Lovers* the pioneer Freudian novel.[1]

Perhaps it is legitimate to pause to consider one set of biographical facts. As Lawrence was rewriting the novel, then called *Paul Morel*, he rather insensitively sent on the revised manuscript to Jessie Chambers, who had found the earlier version tired and removed from reality. The revised draft "bewildered and dismayed" her by its treatment of Miriam. "The shock of *Sons and Lovers* gave the death-blow to our friendship," she says.[2] They never saw each other again. Indeed, there have been many in later years who cannot forgive Lawrence for betraying the love and trust of a fine and sensitive woman. Lawrence's defense, in a projected preface to his *Collected Poems*, is not totally disingenuous in its differentiation between the obligations of genius and of the ordinary man. Miriam, he says, "encouraged my demon. But alas, it was me, not he, whom she loved. So for her it was a catastrophe. My demon is not easily loved: whereas the ordinary me is. So poor Miriam was let down. Yet in a sense, she let down my demon, till he howled. And there it is."

Part I of the novel provides a generous background for the later depiction of Paul Morel's psychological bondage. Three constants of Lawrence's thought appear almost immediately: a lament for the deterioration of the natural environment as a result of industrial process; a strong sense of social inferiority and a determination to break the shackles of class; and an awareness of the conflict between the sexes, in marriage and out, which betrays itself in such chapter titles as "Strife in Love" and "Defeat of Miriam." The first two responses are only incidental accompaniments to Paul's development. The main thrust of the novel is to provide a portrait, not of the artist, but of a young man caught in the confusion of sexual motive and emotion.

The mines of the Bestwood area, on the border of Derbyshire and Nottinghamshire, had been in existence for 200 years in a small way when the growth of nineteenth-century industrialization led to exploitation on a large scale. To accommodate the influx of mineworkers tenements were put up, premises that had solidity and convenience but were so unconcerned for aesthetic needs that the inhabitants looked out not on greenery but on a shambles of backyard litter. To Mrs. Morel, living there is a "struggle with poverty and ugliness and meanness." This constriction of life extends to commercial life as well. Paul, seeking work at the age of fourteen, feels that he is already "a prisoner of industrialism." The premises of the manufacturer of surgical appliances are "like a pit," an image linking them with the mines from which he is seeking to escape.

Reenforcing this physical alienation is a sense of social inferiority, arising from the disparate origins of Walter and Gertrude Morel. The husband, who had gone into the pits at the age of ten, is barely able to read and write. His manners at table may be those of the natural man, but they are deplorable. He lives pretty much from day to day, not irresponsible so much as content to accept the limitations of his lot and expecting his sons to follow the same pattern. His wife had grown up in a middle-class background, had been an assistant teacher, and was considered "very intellectual." Her speech was Southern, not Midlands, "a purity of English" that thrilled Morel when he was courting her. She had no notion in advance of the economic and social deprivation she would suffer as Morel's wife. When she realized that her situation would not change, she devoted her energies to seeing that her children escaped. She feels great satisfaction when her son William is launched and begins to associate with the bourgeois of Bestwood. There is satisfaction also when he makes a go of it in London, even though he stops sending money home. But there is humiliation when he brings his girl—a real lady—home for a visit; she expects to be waited on and is conscious of slumming it in the miner's house.

It is against this background of aspiration and disappointment that the sexual combat of Gertrude and Walter Morel takes place. The crux of the matter is that "in seeking to make him nobler than he could be, she destroyed him." This lofty judgment by the narrator is made concrete by a process that is down-to-earth in its bitter daily skirmishes. Morel was "soft, non-intellectual, warm," with a "sensuous flame of life." She had "a high moral sense" inherited from her Puritan forebears. She was almost a religious fanatic in her attempts to reform him, and these attempts, in his opinion gratuitous, drove him deeper into the faults she wished to correct.

The beginning of the novel abounds in instances of this battle. Morel cuts off the curls of their first child, William: he will not allow his wife to make a wench of the boy. Even though Mrs. Morel apologizes for her anger, this event marks the beginning of estrangement. After a day in the country with a pal Morel comes home drunk. When his wife

turns on him, he calls her "a nasty little bitch" and
forces her out into the August night. It is hours before she can rouse him from his stupor to unlock the
door. Her one solace in her deprived situation is to
entertain the Congregational clergyman. Morel on
one occasion comes home weary and dirty and irritable. He goes out of his way to affront the minister
by his talk and manners. After the minister leaves
there is a domestic brawl underlined by the heavy
irony of William's reading the motto over the fire-
place: "God Bless Our Home." In another fight, after Paul's birth, Morel throws a table drawer at his
wife and cuts her face. He is immediately repen-
tant, but his wife stores away memory of the incident as further fuel to her hatred and aversion. All
these incidents lead to "a deadlock of passion" between them, in which she is the stronger and the
more obdurate.

Though she hardened in her overall attitude toward her husband, there is a degree of ambivalence
in her feeling toward him. She had intermittent pe-
riods of tenderness, or at least of acceptance. When
she had to nurse Morel through a long illness, "she
never quite wanted him to die. Still there was one
part of him she wanted for herself." She became
more tolerant of him, perhaps because she loved
him less. She did have another child, Arthur, by
him, but nonetheless she was relentlessly, if regret-
fully, casting her husband off.

The oldest son, William, accepted his mother's
devotion and high expectations without being psychologically shackled by them. In due time he escaped to London, without considering that "she
might be more hurt at his going away than glad of
his success." His sudden death almost killed Mrs.
Morel. Shortly afterward, Paul, now sixteen, came
down with pneumonia and was in bed for seven

weeks. At night his mother lay with him; it comforted him to put his head on her breast. Concern for Paul saved Mrs. Morel's life, which then became rooted in him even more tenaciously than it had been in William. It was a devotion that would cripple and threaten to destroy her son.

So much for the leisurely background to the main action of the novel, which is Paul's struggle as a young man to find his way to sexual maturity and fulfillment. There are four major participants in this action: Paul, Mrs. Morel, Miriam Leivers, and Clara Dawes, a married woman living apart from her husband. As is characteristic of Lawrence's fiction, the novel ends inconclusively. It is the movement to that nonconclusion that is engrossing and instructive.

Of necessity some attention is given to Paul in the first part of the work, but more to the circumstances of his life than to the personality shaped by them. We learn of his sensitivity and of his emerging talent as artist. Because of his anguish over his mother's suffering from her conflict with his father he early develops an unusual awareness of the feelings of others. He is not involved in the rough and ready play of the collier children. Early shyness, illustrated by a scene in which he collects his father's pay at the pub, pushes him toward communion with nature. He is not soft, not a sissy in the usual sense of the word. Neither is he an intellectual in embryo. He is an isolate, prickly in his relations with others, but potentially warm and responsive. This is the young man who is drawn into the life of the Leivers family at Willey Farm when he is sixteen. He is at ease there in what is a fairly normal family situation of give and take. Surprisingly, he gets along well with the Leivers boys and enjoys working with them in the fields.

The figure of Miriam is slow in coming into focus. From her mother she derives a tendency to the romantic and the mystical. At fourteen she is shy and withdrawn. She seeks learning out of pride, in an attempt to define herself on a higher level. Paul loves—and comes to hate—her state of exaltation. But he participates in it, seeing Miriam in dreamy, romantic terms. He helps her with her studies, particularly French, which is a way of saying that they do not meet on a level of ordinary discourse.

A scene that occurs while Paul is staying at the farm after his illness is premonitory of the way things will go for the young couple. As is frequent with Lawrence, the scene is underplayed and takes on meaning only by the accumulation of later bits in the mosaic. Miriam shyly inducts Paul into the secret pleasures of her life. One afternoon she takes him out to her homemade swing. He suggests that she have the first turn. She refuses, almost for the first time taking pleasure "in giving up to a man." At his insistence she eventually takes a turn, though she confesses that she doesn't much care for it. As Paul controls the rhythm of the swinging, she feels his domination "and the exactly proportionate strength of his thrust, and she was afraid." This sexual imagery does not bode well for the pair when they become lovers. She feels the warmth of his flame, but something in her makes her draw back. He is drawn to her "because of the intensity to which she roused him," but she repels him too.

The character of Mrs. Morel, as we have seen, was established in Part I. The repetition of patterns of behavior in the second part seems merely to confirm what the reader already knows. Yet there is a subtle reversal of judgment of this indomitable woman as the novel proceeds. From appearing as victim of an inferior and insensitive husband, she begins to stand out as victimizer, by her intransigence destroying her husband and putting barriers in her son's way.

The tug of war within Paul between his mother and Miriam is early set forth. As artist, he drew the strength to produce from his mother but needed the delicacy and intensity of Miriam's insight. She, in turn, needed his validation of her own feelings. She knows that a wild rosebush that she has discovered is wonderful, but she cannot accept her feelings until Paul has also seen it. Moreover, standing before the bush with him is a way for them "to have a communion together." Properly responsive on this occasion, Paul in a happy metaphor likens the roses to butterflies. But the scent of the roses, their "white virgin scent," makes him feel "anxious and imprisoned." He wants to get away. He is beginning to discern what his mother has uttered against Miriam with outright hostility: "She is one of those who will want to suck a man's soul out till he has none of his own left." Paul is taken aback when his mother's innate Puritanism makes her burst out that "it is digusting—bits of lads and girls courting." Then he kisses her lovingly and the image of her face and hair blots out that of Miriam.

It is clear to the reader long before it begins to occur to the protagonists that theirs is doomed to be a sterile relationship. Both Paul and Miriam are late in reaching sexual maturity. Without the urgent impulsion of sex Paul is content to "take his pitch from her, and their intimacy went on in an utterly blanched and chaste fashion." Miriam dreams vivid dreams of him. She knows that love is God's gift, and yet it causes her shame. She decides that if she gives herself to Paul it will be as God's sacrifice. Paul is helpless against this semimystical attitude.

He doesn't know that he wants physical fulfillment and can't even bring himself to kiss the girl. She seems to want to make him despise himself for desires that he has not fully formulated in his consciousness. He complains that she wants to make him spiritual, and he does not want to be spiritual. Yet he is afraid of her love: "It was too good for him." In unconscious opposition to Miriam's spirituality, he requires her to read Baudelaire and Verlaine, whose nonspiritual imagery and analysis of love repel her.

It is at the end of the chapter "Strife in Love," at the midpoint of the novel, that the central situation is expertly dramatized. Paul and Miriam have been left to watch the bread baking in the oven one evening while Mrs. Morel is out. They are inattentive and the loaves are scorched, one badly. Paul feels guilty, yet somehow glad: "For some inscrutable reason it served Miriam right." As he reads over her French composition with its barely concealed avowal of love, he is afraid. He sees the yearning in her eyes, begging for a kiss. He knows that before he can kiss her "he must drive something out of himself. And a touch of hate for her crept . . . into his heart." When Paul returns after taking Miriam home, his mother greets him in silence. He apologizes for the bread. Mrs. Morel says she knows the bread was spoiled because he was "engrossed with Miriam." Moreover, she was taken faint carrying the groceries home and Paul should have been there to help her. He defends himself by saying that he and Miriam are interested in things that do not interest Mrs. Morel. She bridles at that, and in exasperation he bursts out: "You're old, mother, and we're young." This hurts her.

As Paul kisses his mother goodnight, she throws her arms around his neck and whimpers that she can't bear it, that Miriam would leave her "no room, not a bit of room," and, pulling out the final stop, she reminds her son: "I've never had a husband—not really—" Paul denies that he loves Miriam. His mother kisses him fervently as he gently strokes her face. Having won, she concedes: "Perhaps I'm selfish. If you want her, take her, my boy." At this point Morel comes in, tipsy after an evening at the pub. His wife's emotion turns into "sudden hate of the drunkard." The two quarrel. Paul wants to fight his father. Mrs. Morel has another fainting spell. When she has regained her strength and prepares to go up to bed, Paul begs her: "Sleep with Annie, mother, not with him." The Oedipal attachment is explicit.

Paul is increasingly outspoken in his irritation and frustration with Miriam. She is "full-breasted and luxuriously formed," but she dreads her body. She "wheedles the soul out of things"; she doesn't want to love but to be loved; she absorbs, in a negative way. Paul complains that their friendship "neither stops there nor gets anywhere else." His inner conflict wears him out. He tries to see less of Miriam and diverts his friendship to her brother Edgar.

At this point Miriam brings Clara Dawes into the picture as a kind of test of Paul's desires for "higher" or "lower" things. Paul is twenty-three, still a virgin. Clara is thirty, a married woman who has lived apart from her husband for some time. She is voluptuously formed. Paul is excited by the swell of her breasts, the molding of neck and arms. When he and Miriam and Clara are out for a walk one day, they speak to a farmer and his spinster sister, who talks rapturously about the stallion they are leading. Clara's judgment is to the point: "she wants a man." A hot wave goes over Paul; he forgets Miriam in his interest in Clara.

Mrs. Morel is not hostile to Clara because she feels the stronger. The two women get along very well when Paul brings Clara to tea one Sunday. When Miriam drops in, she receives the final blow of seeing Clara accepted in a way that she has never been.

Before this open defeat by Mrs. Morel, Miriam has finally yielded sexually to Paul, perhaps as the result of a letter he sent her when she became twenty-one, characterizing her attitude as that of a nun: "In all our relations no body enters." As Miriam contemplates surrender, her whole body resists involuntarily. As she had foreseen, when Paul takes her for the first time, in the woods, her feeling is one of immolation, and a kind of horror. Paul finds himself "physically at rest, but no more." He lies unsatisfied and sad on the dead leaves with a "strange, gentle reaching out to death."

The young couple go to stay alone at her grandmother's cottage, where the rite of sacrifice is repeatedly enacted. Paul wears Miriam out with passion, and she admits that she really doesn't like it. Her mother had told her how it would be. He offers marriage; she draws back. Sometimes he hates her but he remains loyal even as he finds reasons to stay away from her. The truth is that "For one day he had loved utterly. But it never came again." He tells Miriam that she should marry one of those men who worship women and put them on a pedestal. She knows that he is fighting a battle to get free of her, but she remains alone within herself, waiting for him somehow to capitulate to her.

Once Paul feels the attraction of Clara, he undergoes all the traditional agonies of lovesick youth. Their first assignation takes them on a dangerous walk along the flooded river bank and then, exhilarated by danger, to a coupling in an open field in view of possible passersby. Their affair is a passionate one, but Paul begins to realize that she too withholds herself in various ways. He concludes that she is "fearfully in love with me, but it's not very deep." Even when they stay together at the seashore and know "the tremendous living flood" that sweeps over them in their lovemaking, Clara feels that she has not got him and is not satisfied. She and Paul in their passion have received the baptism of life, "but now their missions were separate." The sex act is the culmination of everything for them. There is nothing beyond it. Paul begins to doubt that he can give himself to anyone. He cannot love in the sense of surrendering to another. And it is that surrender, that dependence, that Clara needs rather than carnal passion of itself, after which she is somewhat ashamed.

It is inaccurate to see Paul's two love affairs as a contrast between sacred and profane love, even though Miriam appears to view it that way. She is prepared to wait until Paul, having sown his wild oats, comes back to his better self. However, the basic pattern is Paul's striving for emotional independence, ultimately from all three women, though in the case of Clara her hold is not strong. He tells Clara, in fact, that when his ship comes in, he will get a pretty house near London and live there with his mother. On the other hand, he tells his mother that he will never meet the right woman for marriage as long as his mother is alive. It is clear enough to him that, even though he now has an independent sexual existence—a first break from his mother's domination—he is by no means free.

The part of the novel in which Clara is central is the least convincing part of the work, since Lawrence has here cut loose from his own experience and has had to invent. The most interesting part of that invention is Paul's relationship with Baxter

Dawes, the husband. Humiliated by Clara's rejection, Baxter beats Paul. In spite of this Paul feels sympathy for him, and later visits him in the hospital when he is ill. Ultimately Paul brings about Clara's return to her husband. Paul is astute enough to see that whether Clara loves Baxter is not of primary importance. She feels sure of him because he depends on her emotionally, something that Paul will never do.

The bondage of son to mother is less easy to resolve. Paul comes back from his seaside vacation with Clara to find that his mother is dying of cancer. Her grim effort to hold onto life parallels her tenacity in her earlier relationship with husband and family. Paul tends his mother devotedly, but in time is overwhelmed by anguish over her suffering and by impatience for the end to come. He and his sister finally give Mrs. Morel an overdose of morphia. Even then she hangs onto life for an agonizing twelve hours. Paul kisses her passionately in death. Free at last, he is completely adrift: "His mother had really supported his life. He had loved her. They two had, in fact, faced the world together." Yet the killing of his mother is not altogether an act of compassion. We must see it also as the striking out of Paul against the person who has held him in subjection. Revenge as well as love is in play.

For a time Paul is dominated by a death wish. Miriam wants to save him by marriage. He resists on the familiar grounds: she loves him so much that she wants to put him in her pocket, where he would smother. In his wavering state of will he later makes an offer. To her question as to whether he really wants to marry, his reply is, "Not much." Miriam is not strong enough to take him on this uncertain basis, and the novel ends unresolved.

Some readers have felt that the summoning up

of resolution to go on living that is Paul's ·final stance is illogical, that the novel has not prepared for this conclusion. Yet the whole tenor of the novel is for life. The forces for life innate in Paul can be seen to take over by default. In any event, the novel is only vaguely affirmative. What Paul will do hereafter, what wholeness of being he may achieve, is left up in the air. The problem of Paul Morel, and by extension of others in a like situation, has been examined and clarified. That is as far as the novel seeks to go. Lawrence's honesty prevents him from capping the demonstration with a consoling and anodyne resolution.

Three observations about technique need to be made in respect to this first major novel. There is, first of all, a noticeable variation in the point of view of the narrator. This is a not unlikely penalty of writing an autobiographical novel. There can be a blurring of emotional tone and judgment when the subject of the life takes over from the impersonal, objective narrator. Sometimes this is a matter of distance merely. A scene or incident is so painfully and indelibly inscribed in memory that it is given a primacy out of harmony with the predominant tone of the work. The critic Eliseo Vivas, for example, finds some of the scenes of family conflict unacceptable because of their intensity. It seems to me that there is no harm, even possibly some gain, in this, though it is true that the novel becomes uneven in texture, some incidents standing out with more immediacy than others. This is particularly true after invention predominates and the later scenes lack the sharpness of earlier ones.

Another problem arising from this uncertain position of the narrator is that characters may not be consistent. This is most notable in the case of Walter Morel. In the beginning he is oaf and ogre. Even the children are against him. But at critical points in the narrative he emerges quite different, a sympathetic and warm human being, for example, when he learns of Paul's prizes for his painting. Psychologically I find this duality of view not only acceptable but advantageous. The mind as it works its way reflectively through past experience does come to have second thoughts, to vacillate in the face of contradictory evidence, to perceive some white beneath the black. In other words, such ambivalence is part of the basic psychological process of the narrative and actually increases its validity. This is very important in the delineation of Mrs. Morel. A change in the narrator's evaluation is necessary to parallel Paul's painful reassessment on a subconscious level. (Frieda quotes Lawrence as saying: "I would write a different *Sons and Lovers* now; my mother was wrong, and I thought she was absolutely right."[3])

The second observation about technique is that Lawrence does not plot his novels in the logical, analytical way of his great nineteenth-century predecessors. There is no neatly geometrical pattern with parallel actions, balancing scenes, and a demonstrably climactic point. Rather the technique is one of assembling pieces of a mosaic in a pattern that, while not random, nonetheless gives the impression of casualness. A better way of putting it is to say that the narrating intelligence, possessed of a comprehensive memory of the events related, assembles them through the nonlogical process of recollection. There is some order in the process, since it is deliberate, but it also entails repetition and violations of temporal and logical order. The problem set is to follow Paul, whose origins are a set of givens, to the point at which the novel leaves him. The solution is to summon up relevant memory,

with the meanderings and omissions that memory
makes. The result is a density and verisimilitude
not often achieved by more formal patterning.
(Edith Wharton, a master of the traditional novel,
was appalled by *Sons and Lovers*, which a friend
had recommended to her attention, calling it "a
botched and bungled piece of work."[4])

The most distinctive technical device is the
third. The reader cannot escape observing the fre-
quency and intensity of the passages describing nature, specifically flowers and flowering things.
There is an awareness of nature in its inspiriting
and nurturing function which constitutes an implicit statement that for a human being to be whole
he must have a proper rapport with nature. This
wholeness, or an aspiration to it, is present in Paul
from early on. It is because of his intuitive sense of a
proper relation that we can accept his opting for life
over death at the end of the novel. His innate nature, in other words, is stronger than imposed psychological patterns.

The passages stressing nature imagery give an
important guide to evaluation of the principal characters. The most memorable episodes are the ones
where this device is used. On that occasion early in
the novel when Morel shuts his wife out of the
house, her anger at her husband is qualified by her
response to the tall white lilies "reeling in the
moonlight," the air "charged with their perfume, as
with a presence." She puts her hands on the flowers,
then shivers. She inhales their scent, which makes
her dizzy. She is, in other words, both attracted and
repelled by the intensity of sex in nature. The incident concludes with the words: "In the mysterious
out-of-doors she felt forlorn."

However, in general Mrs. Morel's response to
nature is sounder than Miriam's. In another early

incident we see the mother outdoors with infant
Paul. She savors the beauty of a Derbyshire sunset:
"it was one of those still moments when the small
frets vanish, and the beauty of things stands out, and
she had the peace and the strength to see herself."
Miriam tends to spiritualize nature, thus destroying
the natural, spontaneous relationship that is good,
as exemplified by Mrs. Morel's response to the
scyllas that turn up unexpectedly in her garden. Miriam, we are told, hates spring, even though she is
drawn to the "blood heat" of the thrush eggs. On his
first walk with Clara, Paul learns that she doesn't
like to pick flowers; she doesn't want their corpses
around her. Miriam decides in her characteristic
way that it's all right "if you treat them with reverence." Paul takes a matter-of-fact position: "You get
'em because you want 'em, and that's all."

The prelude to Paul's and Miriam's first sexual
embrace is a detailed nature vignette. He is high in
a cherry tree gathering the ripe fruit. She is on the
ground, where the skeletons of four dead maraud-
ing birds are laid out. In the tree Paul sees stems
consisting only of cherry pits that have been picked
clean like skeletons. He pelts Miriam with cherries
and she hangs a pair of them over each ear. This
double image is very effective. For a moment she is
one with nature in natural and spontaneous response. But underneath is fear and denial, an equat-
ing of nature with death—death of the spirit, no
doubt—as suggested by the previous image. This is
the attitude that accompanies her yielding to Paul a
few minutes later in a setting dominated by dead
leaves.

The most impressive instance of all occurs on
the evening when Paul decides to break with Miriam. He is drawn out of doors by the scent of the
madonna lilies into the night glowing with the light

of a half moon. The scent of the flowers intoxicates him pleasantly until "like a shock, he caught another perfume, something raw and coarse." It is the purple iris with fleshy throats that "stood stiff in the darkness" and whose "scent was brutal." This underside of nature, this phallic aspect, which is just as important, just as much a part of life as moonglow and madonna lilies, is what his relationship with Miriam lacks, and will continue to lack.

The attentive reader will early become aware of this superaddition of nature imagery at critical points in the narrative. Like all image patterns it is to a degree unnatural, but the test is rather the degree to which it appears spontaneous and naturally emergent from narrative incident. As I have suggested, with Lawrence it works both as an overall statement of the importance of a right relationship with nature and as a commentary on persons and events within the novel. It is both a constant and a variable. It is not strident, though ultimately by repetition it does become insistent. It heightens the novel's meaning without diminishing its credibility as everyday experience.

When *Sons and Lovers* was published in 1913, there was no novelist in England or America equal to Lawrence in his power to make readers live in the world of his fiction. The author never again received so spontaneous an acclamation, in spite of the fact that William Heinemann, his previous publisher, thought *Sons and Lovers* "one of the dirtiest books he had ever read"[5] and turned it down. Perhaps that refusal should have forewarned Lawrence. Never again did his novels gain so wholeheartedly favorable a reception.

3

●●

The Rainbow

As he was writing *The Rainbow*, Lawrence commented to his friend David Garnett that "it's all analytical—quite unlike *Sons and Lovers*, not a bit visualized," and said that it went a stratum deeper in probing human psychology than anyone had ever before gone in a novel. This self-congratulatory assessment may be pardoned in the heat of the writer's enthusiasm for his latest offspring. And in fact it is evident that Lawrence was here trying to do something quite different from what he had done in his previous novel, however badly or well it came off.

The concept on which this novel rests is an ambitious one. It seeks to portray the struggles for fulfillment of members of the Brangwen family in three successive generations—during roughly the last half of the nineteeth century, from the coming of the railroad to the Boer War. This approach is essentially deductive, rather than inductive, as was the case with *Sons and Lovers*. It starts with the premise that the pressures of modern society make psychosexual adjustment increasingly difficult, and it carries with it a warning of the decline of the contemporary European man. This design is, in fact, so ambitious that Lawrence could not work it out in a single novel. He continued his analysis of his third-generation characters into *Women in Love*, which, however, is self-subsistent and by no means merely a sequel to *The Rainbow*.

The locale of this novel is typical Lawrence country. Marsh Farm, where the Brangwens have lived for generations, is on the Derbyshire-Nottinghamshire border. As they till the soil, the Brangwen men can look up at the Ilkeston church tower and at the dim smoking hill of town and collieries. Long established on the land, the Brangwens have never become rich. They have lived in proper relation with the land, yielding to its cycles, subordinating self to service.

They felt the rush of the sap in spring, they knew the wave which cannot halt, but every year throws forward the seed to begetting, and, falling back, leaves the young-born on the earth. They knew the intercourse between heaven and earth, sunshine drawn into the breast and bowels, the rain sucked up in the daytime, nakedness that comes under the wind in autumn, showing the birds' nests no longer worth hiding. Their life and interrelations were such; feeling the pulse and body of the soil, that opened to their furrow for the grain, and became smooth and supple after their ploughing . . . They took the udder of the cows, the cows yielded milk and pulse against the hands of the men . . . They mounted their horses, and held life between the grip of their knees, they harnessed their horses at the wagon, and, with hand on the bridle-rings, drew the heaving of the horses after their will.

The farm women have felt this "drowse of blood-intimacy," but they have also looked out "from the heated, blind intercourse of farm-life, to the spoken world beyond." The opening image of Ilkeston church tower is apposite: the men tend to look down at the fields where they work; the women look up at something higher to which to aspire. At any rate, there is a dual movement in the souls of these beings leading the immemorial life of the soil. Their existence cannot remain static. The problem is to maintain harmony in change.

The two Brangwens whom we briefly encounter as progenitors, Alfred and his wife, "were two very separate beings, vitally connected, knowing nothing of each other, yet living in their separate ways from one root." Opinion will vary as to whether this is an ideal condition, but it is a viable one. Many will do worse, and the novel strains toward the possibility of doing as well, or better.

Of this couple's six children it is Tom, the youngest, on whom responsibility for the farm falls when he is eighteen and blessedly released from attending grammar school, where he was "an unwilling failure from the first." At nineteen he has his first experience of sex, with a prostitute. The experience is disillusioning, for his desire is "to find in a woman the embodiment of all his inarticulate, powerful religious impulses." For ten years he is tormented by unfulfilled sexual desires and resorts to bouts of drunkenness to dull the torment. Then one day he sees a Polish woman on the road. This exotic is a refugee, a widow with one small child, who has found refuge as the vicar's housekeeper.

Their union seems predestined. She sees a good body and a healthy stability in Tom. Instinct leads her to accept him for safety and for life. He feels "the strange, inviolable completeness of the two of them." They come together "in an elemental embrace beyond their superficial foreignness." In their day-to-day relationship there is severance, even hostility, but this is healed by fusion in sex. Tom Brangwen shows considerable native tact in dealing with his foreign wife and stepchild. But after the birth of their first child, their sexual life is undermined. She is emotionally absorbed by the new child; he is jealous. She says he does not take her as a man should and resents what she considers his impersonal coupling. He resents giving himself to her completely, but eventually he allows himself to flow to her, again to fuse with her, with the result that after two years of marriage their coming together is more wonderful than in the beginning. In this re-established union the stepchild, Anna, also is secure. She no longer feels responsible for upholding the broken end of the arch of marriage. The parents now meet in a solid span and she is free to play securely beneath it.

It is borne in upon the reader that these are archetypal figures, monolithic, larger than life. This impression is enhanced by the rapt, quasi–Old Testament language that is used, especially in the first part of the novel, suggesting myth rather than closely observed reality. We need to know little more about this couple. They are set in the distance, static, idealized. They function chiefly as an emotional backdrop for the developing Anna, whose generation will provide the next set of exemplary figures.

The second phase of the novel shows the marriage of Anna Lensky to her stepfather's nephew, Will Brangwen, after several chapters relating her development. As she matures, she realizes that her parents and her two brothers make up "a curious family, a law to themselves, separate from the world, isolated, a small republic set in invisible bounds." Anna must break out of these bounds, find her identity in a larger world. She does this with difficulty, since she shrinks from commonplace people, who limit her and force her to define herself falsely. Her ideal, somewhat romantic, as suits her age, is to be "a free, proud lady, absolved from the petty ties, existing beyond petty considerations."

Her cousin Will comes to work at Ilkeston at a fortunate time, when Anna begins to feel the outside world hovering on the edge of her consciousness. He with his passion for church architecture is a kind of exotic. She sees in him an avenue of escape from the circumscription of her own world. Their courtship is rapid—an avowal of love in the chicken loft that is both funny and tender, and a kind of mating dance in the moonlight as they shock up the wheat. They decide to marry in a sort of rapture, ignoring the practical world of money and the prosaic needs of their own natures.

The account of the young couple's honeymoon is the most passionate depiction written by Lawrence up to this point in his career. Anna and Will do not go away but seclude themselves in their cottage next to the church at Cossethay. They ignore night and day and conventional society as they plunge into their lovemaking. For Will marriage is a new beginning: "Suddenly like a chestnut falling out of a burr, he was shed naked and glistening onto a soft, fecund earth, leaving behind the hard rind of worldly knowledge and experience." "Here at the centre the great wheel was motionless . . . Here was a poised, unflawed stillness that was beyond time."

This stasis does not last—is not supposed to last. Anna is the first to need stretching out to the world again. Will does not understand this need. Since he had yielded himself up to her, "There could be only acquiescence and submission, and tremendous wonder of consummation." She cannot understand the passionate intensity—like that which he also has for the church, for the experience of the infinite, the Absolute—of his relationship with her.

There is a beautifully realized account of their sparring as a young married couple, quarreling over such trivial matters as his tools and the mess she makes with her sewing. They fight an unconscious battle in a seesaw of love and conflict. At issue is the fact that they are "separate people with separate destinies," each seeking to lay "violent hands of claim" on the other. In addition, there is the fact that to him she seems self-sufficient, complete, while to his shame he has to acknowledge "his helpless need of her." Anna in turn feels that his will is fastening on her "as a leopard clings to a wild cow and exhausts her and pulls her down." Gradually she realizes that her life, her freedom, are sinking under the silent grip of his physical will. During her first pregnancy she draws away from him, celebrating her new being in a rapturous naked, almost bacchanalian, dance. However ironically we are to take the chapter title, "Anna Victrix," it is with the birth of her first child, Ursula, that she consolidates her victory and places Will in a posture of begging inferiority.

Two encounters aid us in understanding Anna in this phase. One is a renewal of acquaintance with her mother's compatriot, Baron Skrebensky, now the vicar of a northern parish. She is fascinated by his male detachment and self-sufficiency: "A woman was thoroughly outside him." She wonders whether she would prefer this detachment to her husband's "diffuse heat . . . his blind, hot youth." She begins to wonder also if the "close Brangwen life" is not stifling her. She sees how her life might be different and wants her own detached existence, "active but absorbed."

Yet she is hostile to Will's particular avenue to detachment. He takes her to see his beloved Lincoln cathedral, which enraptures him and takes him out of himself. To him the cathedral is "away from time . . . spanned round with the rainbow, the jewelled gloom folded music upon silence, light upon darkness, fecundity upon death." In short, it is an embodiment of the Absolute in its enfolding and reconciling of opposites. The totality of Will's absorption is described in terms of sexual consummation and also as being "at the apex of the arch," which brings in again the persistent rainbow imagery of the novel.

Anna is silenced by, rather than attuned to, the cathedral. To her the religion which it enshrines seems dead: "She claimed the right to freedom above her, higher than the roof." To avoid being swept away uncritically into the infinite in the manner of her husband, "she caught at little things," notably the sly little carved faces in the vaulting that punctured and denied the Absolute. Will is angry because for the moment she destroys his passion for the cathedral. They both go away somewhat altered by the experience: "She had some new reverence for that which he wanted," and he "had lost his absolute." In the long run, Will learns to submit to his wife, who "forced him to the spirit of her laws, whilst leaving him the letter of his own." He has to accept his limitations, to accept "a darkness in him which he could not unfold, which would never unfold in him."

The novel does not indicate when the young couple failed in their relationship, or if it would have been possible for them to avoid failure. It merely shows them mired down in a condition far beneath the ideal, in which husband and wife would be both self-subsistent and fused. Anna gives herself over to a "violent trance of motherhood," eventually having nine children. At twenty-eight Will, having had sexual experience only with Anna, abandons himself to sensuality. He has no interest in his sexual partner as a person but seeks only the intensity of gratification. Anna is aware of this new tendency in Will and rather likes him for it because the change gives her freedom: "He was the sensual male seeking his pleasure, she was the female ready to take hers: but in her own way." Together they abandon any concern for morality in sex and seek gratification pure and simple in "a sensuality violent and extreme as death," finding that these "shameful, natural and unnatural acts of sensual voluptuousness" have "their heavy beauty and delight."

There is little more to say about this marriage. Both partners are prisoners of their own incompleteness. A little perspective is provided by the dramatic interlude of old Tom Brangwen's death, which brings in Anna's half-brother, Tom, who by authorial fiat has "the black depths of disintegration in his eyes." Most important are the ruminations of Brangwen's widow. She wants to withdraw from "The old brutal story of desire and offerings and deep, deep-hidden rage of unsatisfied men against women." She knows that her first husband, Lensky, had failed: "He had lain with her, but he had never known her," and had never let her be herself. Tom Brangwen, however, had given her being and had become one with her in a natural, unstriving way.

This transitional scene of old Tom Brangwen's death is the most gripping in the novel, but by its detail and emphasis it provides a disconcerting alteration in scale and distance. The mythic figure belatedly takes on intensity of being; we identify closely with him when, returning from a day at the market in Nottingham, he is caught in a sudden flood and drowns. In a very real sense the episode is both too graphic and too senseless to belong in the novel.

By its intrusiveness this scene does serve to

mark a basic shift in the novel's course. It abandons static and distanced portraiture and henceforth becomes detailed and personal in its examination of the development of Ursula Brangwen, who represents the third generation in the triptych. Indeed, for the rest of the novel attention shifts from examination of marriage to analysis of the psychosexual development of a young girl before marriage, though marriage again becomes the subject in the ensuing *Women in Love*.

The second half of the novel proceeds topically and somewhat mechanically, as it follows Ursula through adolescence and early maturity. As a child, she early distinguished between the worlds of her parents. Her whole life was directed by an awareness of her father. When he bullied or scolded her, she was crushed but learned to take refuge "in the separate world of her own violent will." The eldest child among a "storm of babies," she is antagonistic toward her mother, who is responsible for the domestic disorder that Ursula hates. She does escape from the constrictions of overwhelming domesticity when she and her sister Gudrun enter the grammar school in Nottingham. The world of knowledge opens up before her: "She trembled like a postulant when she wrote the Greek alphabet for the first time." School subjects are like a bugle calling her to new heights. At the same time this entry into a new world exposes her to new people, hostile people, a mob "lying in wait for her, who was the exception."

At this stage religious feelings and aspirations are paramount in Ursula. She does not like Evangelical teaching with its emphasis on the divinity of Christ—a concept that she feels is the product of vulgar minds. She resents emphasis on death in the reenactment of the Resurrection, since resurrection means coming back to life. She has trouble living in two worlds, one of eternal truth, the other of everyday fact. The weekday world triumphs over the Sunday world as she recognizes the futility of selling all and giving to the poor, or of turning the other cheek. In fact, she finds "something unclean and degrading" about the humility of Christianity.

The religious feelings Ursula experiences are really in response to a sensual need. And it is under their impulsion that she turns to the first emissary from the wider world who touches her life closely. Anton Skrebensky is the soldier son of her grandmother's Polish compatriot in a late marriage. Ursula is entranced by his completeness of being, his acceptance of self beyond question or expectation of change. During the months that Skrebensky is in the neighborhood they are "lovers in the first wondering state of unrealisation." Ursula, without yet giving way, is fascinated by the "world of passions and lawlessness." As they play at kisses, she challenging, he accepting, they are "playing with fire, not with love." This emotional stirring up is "a magnificent self-assertion" by each of them. He feels himself "infinitely male and infinitely irresistible"; she feels herself "infinitely desirable, and hence infinitely strong." Yet in the view of the narrator, who now intrudes, there is something finite and sad about all this.

Throughout this early courtship there is evidence of incompatibility. Their attitudes toward war clash. He is largely oblivious of class structure. Skrebensky's "life lay in the old established order of things . . . The greatest good of the greatest number was all that mattered." In other words, his mind is full of clichés; his actions are safe and indicate no likelihood of expansion or growth. In fact, the two inhabit hostile worlds. Yet this fact is covered up by

the rituals of courtship. He is gratified by her public
show of affection. She restores his shell of compla-
cency by adoring compliance. She knows that she
has him under control, that she has broken him.
Then she perceives in him a kind of nullity that ter-
rifies her.

When Skrebensky goes off to the Boer War, Ursula is thrown back again upon her school for stimulus. She sees education as a means to social and personal independence, to adventuring into and
conquering "the mysterious man's world." She is attracted to Winifred Inger, one of her teachers, a
modern young woman of twenty-eight who is
"proud and free as a man, yet exquisite as a woman."
"A queer awareness" grows up between them. Ursula thrills to the touch of her teacher in the swimming pool. On a weekend together at the seashore
they go swimming in the nude at night. Ursula feels
shame, then a renewed and urgent attraction. For a
time she is with the older woman as much as possible. Then after the school year is over a kind of nau-
sea comes over her. Ursula refuses to go to London
with Winifred, but later she does consent to go with
her to stay with Tom Brangwen, who has become
manager of a colliery. Tom has reached "a stability
of nullification," we are told, and promptly finds
in Winifred "a kinship with his own dark corruption." By Lawrentian logic they deserve each other.

This episode presents the most overt social criticism of the novel. The mining town in which Tom
lives is new and raw, with "no organic formation."
The miners find it easier to adapt to the demands of
the mines than to assert their will against them. The
result is that the mines own them. This condition
exists also in office and shop. What a man becomes
is a meaningless lump, an emasculated standing
machine. Ursula, an appalled observer, disowns the

colliery and wants to smash the machine. Her Uncle Tom, on the other hand, is only free when he is serving the machine.

Home once more after her schooling is over, Ursula again fights her mother, who is now pregnant with her ninth child at the end of a "long trance of complacent child-bearing." Ursula tries to strike out by herself and is offered a post at a school in Kingston-on-Thames. Her parents refuse to let her go so far away but do finally allow her to take a less desirable job in Ilkeston. There she finds that she has stepped unprotected and unprepared into the man's world for which she has yearned. The narrator comments, in strict Wordsworthian terms, that "The prison was round her now!" Her teaching experience is sheer drudgery mixed with horror. She has to go against the grain of her nature and become "a hard, insentient thing, that worked mechanically according to a system imposed." She soon discovers that she will never be much of a success as an elementary teacher, but in her pride she is determined not to be a failure. She hates the job and all it entails, but she manages to survive.

There is a period of change in the Brangwen family, which removes from Cossethay to Beldover. Will has resumed the woodcarving that he had given up with marriage and becomes a teacher of crafts. He has not changed: living close to Anna, he is always suffused "with physical heat," moving "from instinct to instinct, groping, always groping on." Ursula is surprised by a proposal of marriage from a young gardener with whom she has been unconsciously flirting. Not only does he have an unsuitable social origin, but his proposal comes during a beautiful moonrise, of which he is oblivious. This fact "separated them infinitely."

The next step in Ursula's quest is for her to go

to the university in Nottingham as a degree candidate, not as a teacher trainee. Her sister Gudrun also goes to art school there.) Again Ursula thrills to the lure of learning, the opening up of new worlds of knowledge. But her excitement dims in the second year. She sees the professors as mere middlemen in an environment of "spurious Gothic arches, spurious peace, spurious Latinity, spurious dignity of France, spurious naïveté of Chaucer." She protests the "sterile degradation of college"; the shining doorways that she approaches from a distance with excitement lead only into another yard that is ugly, dirty, and dead. "She could only stiffen in rejection, in rejection. She seemed always negative in her action." The positive elements of her nature are dark and unrevealed, like a seed buried in dry ash. In her dissatisfaction she knows only that life must be more than mechanical energy and self-preservation and self-assertion. To be oneself is to escape the finite and in some way to achieve oneness with infinity.

After six years of absence, the latter part spent with the army in India, Skrebensky returns. He is now even more alien to Ursula's nature than before; he is so "made up of a set of habitual actions and decisions" that his inner being is inaccessible to her, but she still responds to "the dark, heavy fixity of his animal desire." Though she goes about in a state of "sensual subconsciousness," she takes her time before allowing sexual consummation, which occurs in the shelter of an oak tree. This is their "final entry into the source of creation," though it will lead nowhere. Still at the university, she, to all intents and purposes, lives with Skrebensky for several months. They go to London and Paris, posing as husband and wife, but he continues to delay marriage. She is ambivalent about accompanying him to

India. She sees through the self-righteousness of
the English governing the Indians for their own
good. Yet she would be glad to leave England,
where "Everything is so meagre and paltry." Running naked on the downs in the joyous dawn, she is
depressed at the thought that in a few hours worka-
day England would be "a blind, sordid, strenuous
activity, all for nothing." Not long before the date set
for the wedding she tells Skrebensky that she will
not marry him.

She does not get off scot free from this period of
dalliance. She fails her examination and is denied a
degree. Now she is torn between the bondage of
being a mem-sahib in an English-ruled colony or
the bondage of teaching again without a degree. As
she and Skrebensky copulate for the last time on the
beach in moonlight, the moon draws her she knows
not where. He has at last come to realize that by the
oppressive force that she exercises over him she
will break his bones, crush his body, obliterate him.
Thus he almost eagerly marries his colonel's daughter and sails for India as scheduled.

Ursula makes one further shift of direction and
purpose that I find out of character. In her pride it is
hard to believe that, even though she thinks she is
pregnant, she would submit to giving up "that other
thing, that fantastic freedom, that illusory, conceited
fulfilment which she imagined she could not have
with Skrebensky." Her dilemma does make her
more understanding of her mother's approach of
"taking the life that was given," instead of arro-
gantly trying to create life to suit herself. In any
case, she writes Skrebensky in apology for wanting
to have the moon in her keeping and offering to
come out to him in India, since it is the woman's
role to submit. Her deep-seated misgivings are symbolized in an ensuing scene, the most powerful in

the novel, in which she finds herself challenged and pursued by horses in a pasture. She escapes from these symbolic forces of primal nature by climbing an oak tree. After this experience she falls ill and struggles in her delirium to define her relation with Skrebensky. To her fevered mind his world was "a compression which enclosed her. If she could not get out of the compression she would go mad."

Fortunately for the resolution of her dilemma Ursula discovers that she is not pregnant after all and that her lover is married. She faces a new period of quest. The novel ends with an image of a rainbow faintly rising above the ugliness of actuality. It is an arbitrary conclusion. Ursula's rapt vision and expectation do not rest on anything more than her imperious nature.

While I am among those who do not find *The Rainbow* as engrossing as either *Sons and Lovers* or *Women in Love*, it is on the whole an impressive piece of work. For one thing, it embodies an effort at objectivity—authorial noninvolvement—that is all too rare in Lawrence's fiction. Here the characters have their being outside the author, though it is easy to see that as usual he has drawn from his youthful experiences in Nottinghamshire and that the portrayal and tone of Ursula's first teaching experience parallel his own. But there is no Lawrence figure in the novel, and the very fact of a female protagonist is testimony to the author's effort to create rather than merely to record. Also there is relatively little authorial comment. Only rarely do we hear what becomes a characteristic railing tone in the later novels.

What the novel lacks is a certain convincing inevitability. As indicated earlier with reference to young Tom Brangwen, what the characters are and what happens to them is too obviously by authorial fiat. I do not feel the internal necessity by which Ursula pursues her uneven course. This lack of internal necessity is acceptable for the two earlier generations, since they are largely static, figures in a frieze. But Ursula is not static. She is a developing personality in whom the lines of causality are either arbitrary or blurred. Certainly it can be argued that the very essence of Ursula is that she is a bundle of conflicting personalities, that the springs of her motivation are often hidden, especially to her, and that she has to make her way against the lies and clichés of conventional mores. Certainly it is also true that we see the people around her almost entirely through her eyes and that these perceptions are necessarily fluid, except where, as in the case of the younger Tom Brangwen, character is arbitrarily fixed in advance of perception.

As we have seen, the design of the novel is faulty. Distance and tone in the second half are at variance with the first. This no doubt robs it of the ultimate impact of a work of art that is both intellectually and aesthetically satisfying. But the closer focus on a single character in the second half of the book does spur our interest, does involve us to a degree that the distanced presentation of the earlier generations does not permit.

The Rainbow is an honest book, and in parts a brilliant one. It is ironical that when it was suppressed six weeks after publication in the fall of 1915, it was the superb sixth chapter, "Anna Victrix," that was cited as giving chief offense. This chapter gives a close account of sexual conflict and reconciliation, especially during the period of Anna's first pregnancy. Feeling the exultation of child-bearing, she determines one afternoon to dance her husband's nullification, to dance to her unseen Lord. "She was exalted over him, before the Lord."

He watched, and his soul burned in him. He turned aside, he could not look, it hurt his eyes. Her fine limbs lifted and lifted, her hair was sticking out all fierce, and her belly, big, strange, terrifying, uplifted to the Lord. Her face was rapt and beautiful, she danced exulting before her Lord, and knew no man.

It is difficult to find anything obscene in this passage, but the publisher, Methuen, was obliged to withdraw all copies from sale and to apologize to the court. Questions were raised in Parliament, but the Home Secretary was evasive, and, because it was wartime and people were preoccupied, no effort was made to defend the book or allow its author a hearing.[1] The shock to Lawrence's pride and his hopes was enormous. He acquired an undeserved reputation for pornography which pursued him to the grave.

4

●●●

Women in Love

Ostensibly a continuation of *The Rainbow*, *Women in Love* is, in fact, almost entirely independent of its predecessor. All that is carried over from the previous novel is the Brangwen sisters, Ursula and Gudrun, now in their late twenties. Even the social milieu is different. We are now among the gentry and the intelligentsia, who are only incidentally inhabitants of the mining Midlands. It does not greatly matter where the novel is set, since the issues raised transcend class and locality. The time scheme is carefully indeterminate. In a preface to the American edition, written in 1919, Lawrence says that while the novel is not concerned with the events of World War I, he wants the bitterness of the war to be taken for granted in his characters.

It must be conceded immediately that the four major characters bear a vague resemblance to—or in some way spring from—D. H. and Frieda Lawrence and Middleton Murry and Katherine Mansfield. Murry later wrote that "the theme, or at least the germ of it," was the relationship of the two couples during the war years, but that he did not see this in the novel as written.[1] It is hard to see Katherine Mansfield in Gudrun, and all that Gerald Crich has in common with Murry is that Birkin offered him a pact of blood brotherhood, as Lawrence

did Murry. We know also that the bohemian Halliday is Philip Heseltine, that Hermione Roddice is
modeled rather closely on Lady Ottoline Morrell,
and Sir Joshua Mattheson less closely on Bertrand
Russell. Beyond these correspondences it is wise to
push the autobiographical content no further. The
novel is fiction, not a biographical source.

Character drawing in *Women in Love* is basically different from that of *The Rainbow*. There the
characters tend to be in a frozen posture, static—
with the obvious exception of Ursula. Here they define themselves in motion—both in inner turbu-
lence and in collision with other egos. They are
fluid, changing, volatile, unpredictable. As many
critics have pointed out, these characters in some
ways resemble those of Lawrence's pet abomina-
tion, Dostoevsky, in their intense psychic energy.
However, the Dostoevskian character is predictably
dichotomized, a walking conflict between self-assertion and self-abnegation, in which either Christian humility or prideful self-destruction *must* be
the outcome. Lawrence's people are less logically
constructed. Their courses do not appear to be foreordained; they must find their way. To be sure, we
early discern the negative principle in Gerald Crich
and Gudrun Brangwen that will end in failure, but
this is less explicitly set forth than it would be in
Dostoevsky.

This manner of characterization in turn accounts for the form of the novel. It has an immediacy lacking in *The Rainbow*. It is predominantly
dramatic, not discursive. We come to know the characters in talk and action in a rapidly changing kalei-
doscope of scenes. Involved in the action and talk,
we have little time to reflect on them. Yet the whole
strategy of the novel is to force such reflection by
the unexpectedness, illogicality, or apparent irrele-

vance of the succession of scenes. There is nothing new about this technique. It is not unlike that of Shakespeare's plays, where one scene qualifies, even contradicts, another without the intervention of authorial commentary. In this novel the relation of parts, however, is not immediately self-evident. The framework is so loose that the reader frequently throws up his hands in admission that he is not certain where the novel is going.

As in *The Rainbow* the subject is marriage, or rather mature sexual relations between men and women. The focus is continually on one or another of four characters: Ursula Brangwen, Gudrun Brangwen, Rupert Birkin, and Gerald Crich. As the narrative develops, they sort themselves out into couples: Ursula and Rupert, Gudrun and Gerald. The first pair eventually get married and achieve considerable harmony. The second pair live together for a time, but the relationship breaks down into such bitterness and futility that Gerald commits suicide and Gudrun apparently goes off to a sterile life in the arty world of Dresden. The pattern, however, is not one of simple contrast. The examination of sexual relations is free ranging without dogmatic conclusion, accumulating meaning through the usual literary devices of parallel, contrast, and symbol.

As the novel opens, Ursula and Gudrun are discussing marriage. Both feel the temptation not to marry but both are secretly fearful of missing something important. They are both living in a state of suspension. Gudrun is the victim of boredom: everything withers in the bud, she says. Ursula, who has returned to teaching, feels that active living has been suspended. Their discontent washes over to the area in which they live. The town of Beldover "is like a country in the underworld," Gudrun says.

On an afternoon walk they stop at the village church to watch the wedding of Gerald Crich's sister. The Crich family pique Gudrun's curiosity: there is something "not quite so precluded in them" as in other people. She is struck by Gerald's "strange guarded look," by something northern in him, "like sunshine refracted through crystals of ice," that sets her "veins in a paroxysm of violent sensation." She determines to see more of him. Ursula, for her part, wants to know more of Rupert Birkin, the best man, whom she has met only professionally in his role of school inspector.

As this casual encounter sets the narrative in motion, it is important to remember that all four characters are mature people, sexually experienced and aware of the ways of the world. Theirs is not the intoxication of first love but a considered exploring of a relationship to see whether it will be sustaining and fulfilling. This permits the action to move slowly and to be buttressed with much talk, much philosophical speculation, before and after eventual sexual consummation.

We learn almost immediately that Birkin is breaking off an affair with Hermione Roddice, a member of the arty, intellectual set, one of "the lack aristocracy that keeps touch with the arts." She is somewhat predatory, needing a man to counter her sense of inadequacy. Her sexual passion is really only will, a bullying will. She wants to clutch things and have them in her power. She has no real body, no real sensuality. Her attitude is pornographic: "watching your naked animal actions in mirrors." She is an example, according to Birkin, of "The vicious mental-deliberate profligacy our lot goes in for." An intellectual, she cannot understand how there can be knowledge that is not in the head. She has no sense of "blood consciousness," of "actual sensual being." It is inevitable that she and Birkin quarrel and break off, since he is a more serious person and has a sense of the possibility of a deeper, more full-blooded relationship.

Echoing Hermione's superficiality is a bohemian group who cluster at the Café Pompadour in London. Birkin, who mingles with them on occasion, introduces Gerald Crich to their circle, in particular to Minette, with whom Gerald goes to bed with the complaisant acceptance of her lover, Halliday, and his friends. For the moment Minette wants "the experience of his male being," in contrast to the twittery effeminacy of Halliday. However, she does not intend to give up her lover permanently. The bohemian set are only half-men, and that is the kind that she can dominate.

These examples of ill-directed sexuality are both allied to and diminished by the sexuality of a primitive carving of a woman in childbirth in Halliday's apartment. It and another African statue are referents throughout the novel for a dark blood consciousness in contrast with the brittleness of modern sensuality. Gerald is repelled by the statue, as he is repelled by the manners of the group, who loll about naked in Halliday's apartment. He wants "to keep certain illusions, certain ideas like clothing." He is disturbed by Birkin's repudiation of standards of behavior for exceptional people. His sensuality is without depth. An avid womanizer, he looks upon his partners as toys and copulates without passion and with no expectation of permanence. He believes in the work ethic. Indeed, as the novel proceeds he comes to stand for the captain of industry who has been dehumanized to the point of being part of the machine. Gerald "is artificially held together by the social mechanism." It is important, however, to see him as an attractive figure. Not

only does he stir Gudrun's sensuality, but he draws
Birkin to him in an aching desire for blood brotherhood.

Birkin, as the reader soon realizes, is a Lawrence figure, a rather beguiling one who can on occasion make fun of his own outré behavior and
ideas. He is a quester and thinker, an idealist in the
first degree. He tells Gerald that he wants "the fi-
nality of love"—one woman who will be the core
and center of his life. Birkin feels there is no other
possible cohesive force than love, "seeing there's
no God," and since "the old ideals are dead as
nails." He is properly sceptical of the vaunted freedom of his bohemian acquaintances. They are
bound by their conformity to nonconformity.

Ursula's attraction for Birkin is not explained.
Spontaneously he finds her to be "a strange unconscious bud of powerful womanhood. He was unconsciously drawn to her. She was his future." Yet he
does not accept that future without a battle. After a
violent altercation with Hermione he goes out for a
walk, removes his clothing and sits naked like Buddha among the primroses, then like a Christian as-
cetic suffers the mortification of fir branches as he
walks among the trees. Soothed by perfect alone-
ness, he sees the error of wanting people, of wanting a woman: "The world was extraneous." Or so he
thought for the moment.

Once the four main characters and Hermione
as a foil have been introduced, the novel proceeds
by a series of encounters, frequently collisions, of
these characters, which develop and define the psychosexual ties between them as they go their ways
toward fulfillment or nonfulfillment. To a degree
Women in Love is a traditional love story, since the
lovers do have to run an obstacle race. But the old
clichés are tossed away (though Lawrence develops

his own clichés) in the interest of a searching examination of the possibilities of love.

In Chapter IX, "Coal Dust," we get the measure
of Gerald and Gudrun, when at a closed railroad
crossing Gerald forces his terrified mare to wait as a
train passes. Ursula thinks him a fool and a bully,
but Gudrun is numbed in her mind at the thought of
the "indomitable soft weight of the man, bearing
down into the living body of the horse; the strong,
indomitable thighs of the blond man clenching the
palpitating body of the mare into pure control." She
generally feels a "resonance of physical men" that is
potent and half-repulsive, as, for example, when she
is stirred by the sight of miners washing after work,
"naked down to the loins." On a later occasion when
she sees Gerald and Hermione out rowing, there is
an exchange of feeling between Gudrun and Gerald
below the level of consciousness, as she stares at
him through "the rigid, naked, succulent stems" of
the water plants. She knows that she has power over
him. In a later encounter, when Gerald grapples
with a frenzied rabbit, both he and Gudrun end up
with bloody scratches, a blood brotherhood that
verifies their psychic bond and in advance defeats
the possibility of blood brotherhood that Birkin
seeks.

Ursula's first significant meeting with Birkin
comes while he is caulking a boat. As usual he uses
her as a sounding board for his ideas. She wants him
to say that the final goal of life is love. He says it is
freedom. Ursula's feelings about him are initially
ambivalent. She sees in him both "the rare quality
of an utterly desirable man" and a Sunday-school-
teacher prig. He tells her that he does not want
love, which "gives out in the last issues." Instead he
wants to meet her "beyond the emotional, loving
plane." He does not want her good looks or wom-

anly feelings or thoughts and ideas. He aspires rather to "a strange conjunction" with her, not "meeting and mingling" but "an equilibrium, a pure balance of two single beings;—as the stars balance each other." It is Birkin's belief that the world is held together by a mystic conjunction in which "the immediate bond is between man and woman." He loves Ursula but he wants something better and beyond love. We learn that in a way he hates sex because "it turned a man into a broken half of a couple, the woman into the other broken half." He abhors the "hot narrow intimacy" between man and wife. This statement, ironically, comes when after being intoxicated by kisses and forgetting his reservations in passion, he wants—and apparently has—Ursula in the "ultimate and triumphant experience of physical passion."

Ursula, deeply in love with Birkin, nevertheless feels that he is "the enemy, fine as a diamond, and as hard and jewel-like, the quintessence of all that was inimical." One night as she walks by Willey Water she observes Birkin shattering the perfection of the moon's image in the water by throwing stones. Breaking in upon his solitude, Ursula tells him that it is horrible to destroy the moon (which in this novel and its predecessor is a symbol, or at least an accompaniment, of sexual passion). She goes on to complain that their relationship is one-sided, that it is not fair that he wants her to serve him but is unwilling to serve her. He in turn wishes she would drop her "assertive will," at the same time realizing that she is "a paradisal bird that could not be netted, it must fly by itself to the heart."

Birkin is prone to decry knowledge through the senses as dissolution and corruption, a death of the creative spirit. He is sure there must be another way, a way of freedom, "the paradisal entry into

pure, single being, the individual soul taking prece-
dence over love and desire for union." Ursula is dubious about "mutual union in separateness." She
wants to have him completely, believing that love
far surpasses the individual, while he believes that
the individual is more than love. It is this opposition of attitudes and feelings that causes Ursula not
to answer Birkin's proposal of marriage and him to
fling away in anger and hurt at her apparent repudiation.

Earlier, in his reaching out for perfection,
Birkin had hoped to find Gerald a possible instru-
ment. In the novel as we have it this development is
sudden and ill prepared. However, in one of
Lawrence's discarded prefaces to *Women in Love*
there is a detailed account of Birkin's feelings prior
to the opening of the novel. He had vacillated between the physical attraction of Gerald and the intellectual attraction of Hermione. In any case,
Birkin now confronts "the problem of love and eternal conjunction between two men," realizing that
he has been deeply attracted to Gerald all along. He
brings up the example of the blood brotherhood of
the old German knights. Gerald asks Birkin to drop
the subject until he understands it better.

It is at this point that the novel provides exten-
sive expository material about Gerald, whose
father's imminent death will leave Gerald "exposed
and unready before the storm of living . . ." In childhood he had rebelled against all authority: "Life
was a condition of savage freedom." Then when he
became manager of the colliery, he developed a
concept of "the pure instrumentality of mankind,"
repudiating humanitarian and Christian ideas of
love and sacrifice. Gerald's position was that
"Man's will was the absolute, the only absolute."
What mattered was the great social productive ma-

chine. Just as he saw workmen as instruments to production, he saw women as instruments of his pleasure, without interest to him as human beings.

Gerald admits to Birkin that he is bored: work, love, and fighting is all there is. Fighting leads to a discussion of Japanese wrestling, in which Birkin has some skill and which he undertakes to demonstrate to Gerald. They lock the door, strip, and after learning the rhythm of each other's body, wrestle "rapturously." The wrestling is described in terms of sexual encounter, Birkin being the aggressive figure who, finally exhausted, passes out on top of Gerald. As they lie semiconscious, there is an involuntary clasping of hands—a temporary acceptance of the brotherhood Birkin has sought. He says the wrestling is good; when they are mentally and spiritually intimate they ought to be physically intimate too. The episode ends in a discussion of love. Gerald, who has had plenty of women, says he has never felt love, never as much for a woman as he feels for Birkin. They both doubt that Gerald ever will feel love. He wants *to be loved*—and fulfilled. Birkin supplies the word. Gerald guesses that is what he wants.

The ambiguity of this scene is interesting. There is a consummation of some kind from which both men draw back. Immediately afterward Ursula gains ascendancy in Birkin's mind. And Gerald by his remarks just mentioned in effect says that the way of blood brotherhood will not enable him to love completely either. Birkin repeats what Gudrun has earlier discerned, that Gerald has a northern kind of beauty, which means that Birkin is aware of his friend's potential for self-destruction.

From early in the narrative Gerald has been identified with water, which in the context of this work seems to be not a source of life, but a source of

death. What Gudrun thrilled to when she first saw
him swimming was actually corruption, a death
wish or an alliance with death. It is Gerald who attempts and fails to rescue his drowning sister, Di-
ana. Even in this crisis Gudrun is mesmerized by
"the beauty of the subjection of his loins" as he fran-
tically dives in search of the girl. The slow death of
Gerald's father is a further subjection to the forces
of dissolution. Being the kind of person who ignores
illness and death, Gerald is at a loss when he must
acknowledge them.

It is in this condition that he reaches out for solace from Gudrun. He tells her that she is everything to him. They embrace under the railway via-
duct just like the miners and their girls. As she
kisses him he likens her to Eve: "The fathomless,
fathomless desire [her fingers] could evoke in him
was deeper than death, where he had no chance."
After his father's funeral he cannot face his own
eventual nothingness. One night he visits his
father's grave at Willey Green church. Then he slips
unseen into the Brangwen house, finds his way by
instinct to Gudrun's room, and tells her he has come
because he must. "Into her he poured all his pent-
up darkness and corrosive death, and he was whole
again." She received him "in an ecstasy of subjection." She was "the great bath of life," "mother and
substance of all life." "Like a child at the breast, he
cleaved intensely to her." As he sleeps, Gudrun
looks at his beautiful, remote, perfected being and
knows that they will never be truly together.

In a scene preceding this climax in the Gerald-
Gudrun affair the Birkin-Ursula relationship also
reaches a peak. He takes her for a drive and gives
her three rings as tentative engagement tokens.
They dispute as usual. Ursula says it may be that his
spiritual brides cannot give him what he wants, but

she warns him not to marry her just for "daily use."
He counters that "spiritual intimacy"—Hermione's
forte—is no rottener than Ursula's "emotional-
jealous intimacy." She throws the rings at him and
walks away. After a while she returns with a flower
in her hand. All is simple again. Birkin's heart is
filled with tenderness, and at tea in a restaurant in
Southwell Ursula kneels and embraces his loins,
feeling the "life-flow." She has had lovers and
known passion but this is something more. "It was
the daughters of men coming back to the sons of
God." Determined to seek freedom together, they
write out resignations from their jobs. They are sure
that somewhere they can be free, somewhere they
will not need to wear many clothes—"none even,"
Birkin hopes—somewhere they can be themselves
without bothering. Instead of going to their homes
that night they drive to Sherwood Forest, where
they pass the night naked in each other's arms.

With both couples having reached sexual
union, the basic question is raised again in Chapter
XXV, "Marriage or Not." The dialogue is between
Birkin and Gerald. Birkin says he is not really interested in legal marriage, which is merely a matter of
social convenience. Gerald reminds him that marriage is a final commitment, implying that it needs
the full sanction of a legal bond. However, he concedes that marriage is only an alternative—to what,
he does not know. Birkin replies that it is merely a
pis aller—a makeshift expedient—and deplores the
fact that it entails a "sort of hunting in couples."
However much he believes in permanent union, he
denies that it is the last word. As we know, he wants
something broader: an *"additional* perfect relationship between man and man—additional to marriage." Gerald feels doomed to marriage but incapable of "any pure relationship with any other soul."

As to Birkin's alternative, if he were able to pledge himself with a man, he would then be able later to pledge himself with a woman in both legal marriage and absolute mystical union. But for him commitment is not possible.

The succeeding chapter, "Chairs," offers a beguiling little vignette. Ursula and Birkin, wandering through a second-hand market, buy a chair, a handsome piece that puts contemporary mechanical production to shame. Birkin inveighs against the tyranny of things; Ursula insists that she wants a place of their own. Birkin prays that they will never have it. Suddenly the chair seems superfluous and a burden. They decide to give it to a young couple who are on the eve of a forced marriage. To Birkin these young people are one more example of modern retrograde humanity: The girl is already dominant. "She had got his manhood," though the young man still retained "a strange furtive pride and slinking singleness" by which to resist "the active procreating female." Once more Birkin tells Ursula that he hankers after "a further fellowship." Her reply is not calculated to soothe him: "You've got me. Why should you need others?" He cannot answer the question. Suddenly they decide to get married next day, the license having been secured some time before.

The final phase of the quadruple relationship comes when Gerald and Gudrun go off together, taking the honeymoon before the marriage, as Gerald puts it. She is somewhat insulted that Gerald takes it for granted that she will accompany him without marriage, and she recognizes that the stability of marriage is good. On their way to Austria the two spend a short time in London, where they go to the Pompadour, even though Gudrun has come to loathe "its atmosphere of petty vice and

petty jealousy and petty art." They meet Minette
and her crowd again, and Gudrun is infuriated by
the malicious reading aloud of one of Birkin's more
pretentious letters. She snatches it from them and
leaves. She has repudiated London and her past
arty life without having anything to put in their
place.

To Birkin marriage is "his resurrection and his
life." On the ship to the Continent he feels that he
and Ursula are "falling through a gulf of infinite
darkness like a meteorite plunging across the chasm
between worlds." For the first time utter peace enters his heart. Joining the other couple at a village
above Innsbruck, they find Gerald "shining like sun
on frost." He is "a whole saturnalia in himself, once
he is roused." Gudrun is also in a heightened state.
She says she feels "übermenschlich," a condition
impossible of achievement in England, where the
damper is never off. The ski village high in the
mountains is Gerald's natural habitat: "This was the
centre, the knot, the navel of the world, where the
earth belonged to the skies, pure, unapproachable,
impassable." He is dominated by a constant passion
that is "like a doom upon him." His lovemaking
reaches an unprecedented peak of intensity. Gudrun in this physical and emotional ambience also
feels at home—and *alone*.

To Ursula, on the contrary, the shining outdoors
is "conscious, malevolent, purposive in its intense
murderous coldness." She hates the unnaturalness
of the snow. Birkin says he could not bear "this
cold, eternal place" without Ursula. They are sustained by the warmth of love in a cold universe. After a few days they have had enough and decide to
go south to Italy, to warmth and humanity.

Late in the novel a new character appears.
Loerke is "a thin, dark-skinned man with full eyes,

an odd creature like a child and like a troll." The
latter comparison makes it mandatory to identify
him with Loki, the Norse god of mischief. He is a
strange, perverse being. He and his male companion Leitner are apparently at the end of an affair and
are not speaking to each other. It develops that
Loerke's real sexual passion is for very young girls;
after age sixteen they are no use to him. There is an
immediate bond of spirit between Gudrun and
Loerke. In him she finds "the rock-bottom of all
life"; he belongs to "the underworld of life"; he is a
"mud-child"; "a gnawing little negation." He is a
sculptor like Gudrun. His theories of art are avant-
garde, separating art from morality, making it her-
metic and amoral.

In the heady atmosphere of the mountains the
affair between Gerald and Gudrun falls apart as
each attempts to dominate the other. Gudrun does,
for a moment, toy with the idea of being ambitious
for them as a couple, thinking of the power that
Gerald, with her help, might acquire and exert. Her
cynicism quickly rescues her from such an ambi-
tion: "The whole coinage of valuation [of rising in
the world] was spurious." Neither one loves the
other. His heart whispers: "If only I could kill her."
She forces him to make love, but "His passion was
awful to her, tense and ghastly, and impersonal, like
a destruction, ultimate." They fight a back-and-forth
battle in which "one destroyed that the other might
exist, one ratified because the other was nulled."
Gudrun repudiates Gerald by announcing publicly
that she is not Mrs. Crich. She turns to Loerke because she wants "the subtle thrills of extreme sensation." She has no further use for Gerald, who has
reached his limit in this respect, but she knows she
has more subtleties ahead. Though Gerald has overcome his desire to kill her, when he comes upon

Gudrun and Loerke picnicking in the snow, he is maddened, knocking Loerke down and almost choking Gudrun to death before revulsion overcomes him: "As if he cared enough about her to kill her . . ." His despair and self-destructive instinct take him away from them and higher and higher into the snow until he freezes to death, finding release in the pure absolute of the shining mountains.

Birkin grieves for his friend and, being Birkin, ruminates over the meaning of it all: "Whatever the mystery which has brought forth man and the universe, it is a nonhuman mystery, it has its own great ends, man is not the criterion." It is up to man creatively to change and develop or the creative mystery will discard him. "Races came and went, species passed away, but ever new species arose, more lovely, or equally lovely, always surpassing wonder. The fountain-head was incorruptible and unsearchable. It had no limits . . . To be man was nothing compared with the possibilities of the creative mystery."

In his grief Birkin exclaims that Gerald should have loved him. To Ursula's question as to what difference that would have made, he answers that those who "dying still can love, still believe, do not die. They still live in the beloved." But Gerald, the denier, is now no more than a dead stallion Birkin remembers: "a dead mass of maleness, repugnant." He tells Ursula that loving each other as they do, they have no need to despair in death. But he promptly upsets her by going on to say that although she is all women to him, "I wanted a man friend, as eternal as you and I are eternal." She considers this "an obstinacy, a theory, a perversity" and tells him that he can't have two kinds of love because that's false and impossible. "I don't believe that" is Birkin's still seeking, final word.

The conclusion, no doubt simplistic when finally reached, is that Gerald and Gudrun are damned. Gerald's way is the way of despairing self-destruction. Gudrun, living, is consigned to a half-world presided over by the likes of Loerke. She has reached a permanent moral and spiritual cul de sac. It is too much to say that Birkin and Ursula are saved. They do have a chance. Out of the continual uneasy debate between them—a sort of dialectic—possibly a higher level of feeling and of being may arise. Birkin hopes so. Ursula just hopes to hold on to Birkin. Certainly the novel is not, finally, stamping its seal of approval on running in couples, on uxorious exclusivity. Smug, enclosed domesticity is not the way. The equipoised polarity of which Birkin spoke earlier remains an ideal. Meanwhile he is unwilling to ignore other possibilities of emotional attachment and fulfillment. The conclusion of the novel, as far as Birkin and Ursula are concerned, is not forced. It is still open-ended.

It is somewhat difficult to reconcile the novel's conclusions with Lawrence's introductory remark for the American edition of 1921. He states that "the creative, spontaneous soul sends forth its promptings," which are "our true fate," which it is our obligation to fulfill. "A fate dictated from outside, from theory or from circumstances is a false fate." Certainly theory is satirized in the cases of Hermione, Sir Joshua, and Loerke, and Birkin escapes disaster by being brought out of his theoretical daze. But it is not clear how the individual can escape having his fate channeled, if not determined, by circumstances. On the one hand, it is an article of faith that Gerald and Gudrun could have been other than they are. On the other, we do not see a real possibility of their being other than they are. They are set from the beginning on a downhill track that they follow with very little hesitation. The question is never will they be saved, but how will they go about being damned.

As for a dimension of the novel about which Lawrence is emphatic in his introduction, its reflection of wartime or postwar emotional disequilibrium, I doubt that a reader today will perceive this as important. Perhaps it is that we have supped too full of horrors since the novel was written to see its mood as one of overwhelming malaise. The war is never mentioned. The anxieties and superficialities of the characters are standard for the twentieth century. They need no specific time-setting. Indeed such specificity undermines the broad purpose of the novel, which is to show the decline of the vital human spirit, Lawrence's most persistent theme.

Women in Love was finished in November 1916 and turned down by Methuen the next month. It was not published until May 1921 by Thomas Seltzer in New York. It narrowly missed the fate of *The Rainbow* on both sides of the Atlantic. The New York Society for the Suppression of Vice tried to have it suppressed. In London *The Times* called it "an epic of vice" that should be banned, the sort of book that might bring "unspeakable disaster" to a boy in his teens.[2]

5

●●●

Lady Chatterley's Lover

By intrinsic literary merit *Lady Chatterley's Lover* does not qualify as a major novel. But its history of denunciation and litigation does enhance its importance. It and Joyce's *Ulysses* became *causes célèbres* in the battle over censorship in English-speaking countries during the first half of this century. Thus it is that *Lady Chatterley* is very likely to be the first of Lawrence's novels to which a new reader turns. This is unfortunate, since he is likely to be disappointed in it both as literature and as pornography.

This was the last major literary undertaking of Lawrence's life. It is probable that, aware of his rapidly deteriorating health, he considered this to be his last chance to take a shot at the enemy. He declared to a friend: "I feel I've had another whack at 'em—a good satisfactory whack . . ." Certain it is that as he worked his way through the three versions of the novel his language became more and more certain to arouse the ire of Mrs. Grundy. There can be no doubt that the novel was a deliberate assault on the citadels of prudery.

Once more the setting is the coal-mining district that Lawrence had known in his childhood. Teparshall is Eastwood, and neighboring towns and country houses are recognizably actual places.

However, this is as far as notation of local life goes.
The miners and their wives are only a sullen backdrop to the sexual triangle of the basic plot. The
time scheme is fairly precise. In 1918 Sir Clifford
Chatterley comes back from Flanders shattered in
body. His management of his coal properties coin-
cides with the postwar depression that undermined
England in the Twenties. The old patriarchal England is gone forever. Cash is the sole nexus and the
only goal of work.

Sir Clifford married Constance Reid, daughter
of a Royal Academy painter, in 1917. They had a
month's honeymoon before he went back to the
front. By 1920 he was pronounced cured, so far as
that was possible, but he remained paralyzed from
the waist down. Inevitably his physical suffering
left "a blank of insentience" in a man whose human
sympathies had not been greatly developed to begin with. He had of necessity to ignore or sublimate
his sexual urges, but in fact sex had not been important to him. He was a virgin when he married. At
that time his wife had exulted that their union was
beyond sex, beyond the demand for a man's physical satisfaction.

Connie had an "aesthetically unconventional
upbringing." In her father's circle "impassioned in-
terchange of talk" was what mattered. Both Connie
and her sister Hilda had lost their virginity by the
time they were eighteen, but didn't think much of
sex. Men might glorify it, but women knew there
was something higher. When men "insisted on sex
like dogs," women had to yield, but they could submit to the act without surrendering their inner free
selves. In Germany the sisters "nearly succumbed
to the strange male power," but they drew back,
"took the sex-thrill as a sensation, and remained
free." In England they mixed with the young Cam-

bridge set that stood for freedom and "a well-bred sort of emotional anarchy."

As Lawrence was writing the novel, his friends advised against making Sir Clifford sexually incapable. This loads the dice unnecessarily. The baronet's emotional impotence is the important thing, the impasse from which Connie finally tries to escape. This is less easy to establish, but we do get a picture of emotional deadness when the couple return to their countryseat at Wragby in the autumn of 1920. The house is grim and dark; the servants superannuated and slow. From the house they can see the chimney of Tevershall pit and "the raw straggle" of Tevershall village. They are subject to the "utter soulless ugliness of the coal-and-iron Midlands," where the air is always foul and there is soot on everything, even the Christmas roses. The people of the village are "as haggard, shapeless, and dreary as the countryside, and as unfriendly." In short, Lawrence has here set up a wasteland as obvious as those of his contemporaries Eliot and Fitzgerald.

The Chatterleys' effort to escape the grim environment takes the path of fashion. Clifford becomes something of a writer. His observation is good, but he lacks empathy, or even sympathy. Thus his writing reflects the shallowness of modern life and psychology. He surrounds himself with artistic figures of the same shallow sort, each of them trying to use the others for self-glorification. Among these is Michaelis, a smart young playwright, clearly modeled on the novelist Michael Arlen. The bitch-goddess success has marked him for her own, and since Clifford wants to prostitute himself to the goddess, he invites Michaelis to stay at Wragby, even though the man is an outsider, a bounder. Connie likes him, and in the emptiness of her life is willing to go to bed with him, so long as Clifford doesn't know. We learn with clinical detail that he reaches orgasm too soon. Connie learns how to keep him in and to achieve orgasm "from his hard, erect passivity." The affair is doomed from the beginning, however; Connie realizes that sexually Michaelis is as dead as Clifford.

There is a good deal of chattering about sex at Wragby. Hammond, a writer, says that interest in sex is "misplaced curiosity." Charlie May sees sex as "just an exchange of sensations instead of ideas," to be taken no more seriously than dancing together. Tommy Dukes, a major-general and a traditionalist, protests against analysis and mental dueling: "Real knowledge comes out of the whole corpus of the consciousness, out of your belly and your penis as much as out of your brain and mind." He sees the current Bolshevism as part of this unhealthy mental activity of forcing ideas on life, against one's deepest instincts. His formula is simple. He believes "in having a good heart, a chirpy penis, and lively intelligence, and the courage to say 'shit!' to a lady."

The old England of traditional ways and blood consciousness is minimally preserved in a remnant of Sherwood Forest on Clifford's estate. The gamekeeper whom he has installed there is one Oliver Mellors, the son of a collier who became an officer during the war and by manner and speech might almost be a gentleman. His first encounter with Lady Chatterley is a bit too pat. She and her husband have been discussing her having a child by another man so as to continue the Chatterley line. We know at once that it is Mellors by whom Connie will have a child, though not, as Clifford thinks of it, by a purely clinical act, like going to the dentist.

The woods become Lady Chatterley's refuge in her discontent. On a walk she meets Mellors and his little girl (he is living apart from his wife), and feels anger and contempt in him and falsity and shallowness in the child. On another walk she comes upon Mellors washing, naked to the hips. She is moved by the sight of his "pure, delicate, white loins," and receives "the shock of vision in her womb." The tensions and frustrations of her unnatural life bring her to the verge of breakdown. Her family intervene and lay down the law to Sir Clifford. Mrs. Bolton, a forty-seven-year-old miner's widow, is engaged to take care of him. Connie begins to untangle her tendrils from Clifford's. Together they are a dying plant. She becomes aware of a physical aversion to her husband as well as a growing hatred toward the world around her. "People are killing the very air," she thinks. Society with its mania for money and love is insane. The lower classes have the same lusts as the rest. In fact, there is only one class nowadays.

Connie discovers a hut in the forest where Mellors keeps his brooding hens. The gamekeeper resents her intrusion, but then a thin tongue of flame flickers in his loins. In spite of Mellors's hostility and occasional mockery Connie keeps returning to the hut. The chicks bring her and Mellors together in tender feeling. One afternoon his loins stir uncontrollably and the two become lovers. In a way he regrets coming back to life: "She had cost him the bitter privacy of a man who at last wants only to be alone." Now he has brought himself into "a new cycle of pain and doom." She realizes that he had been kind to the *female* in her—the first time that this had ever happened to her.

The physical encounters ripen into love. One day Mellors finds her in the forest and takes her on a bed of boughs. To her the sensation is like bells rippling inside her. The second time they climax together—something very special, Mellors tells her. Connie's changed appearance, her radiant well-being, leads Mrs. Bolton to surmise that she has a lover, and when early one morning she sees Mellors watching the house, she knows. Fortunately her antagonism toward the ruling classes makes her half side with Connie. Clifford is, of course, oblivious. There is exquisite irony when he reads Racine to her in French and extols the classic control of the passions.

Chapter XI contains a long discursive passage that is less a digression than an antiphonal theme. Connie, going by car to Tevershall and then on into the country, sees nothing but ugliness and vulgarity, the "grey, gritty hopelessness of it all." She feels that "the living intuitive faculty" is dead in these people. Fellowship is dead. The new England is blotting out the old. The great industrial works are the modern Olympia, with temples to all the gods. The streets of the villages once used to lead out to "the wide open world of the castles and the stately couchant homes," but now the stately homes are being pulled down. Squire Winter's Shipley is broken up after his death, and becomes the Shipley Hall Estate, that is, a housing development. The younger generation is not even aware of what is being lost: "There is a gap in the continuity of consciousness, almost American: but industrial really." When Connie asks herself what will come next, she almost believes there will be no next. Again she sees the people as "incarnate ugliness," as "animals of coal and iron and clay . . . The anima of mineral disintegration." This feeling of hopelessness is later tempered on a sunny spring morning when Connie feels "a quiver in her womb too, as if the sunshine had touched it and made it happy." The mawkishness of this statement is unfortunate, but the point is an important one, that Mellors has come from this ugly, soul-extinguished mining community, and that his union with Connie is one of life and hope and human awareness.

Full spring brings mounting passion. One evening she seeks Mellors out at his cottage. At first, when he learns of her plans to have a child, he thinks she is making use of him. Then they go to the hut and for the first time remove all their clothing. They make love three times with an increasing sense of completeness in each other. She feels newly born as a woman, and she has touched his deepest feelings, so that it is as if the sons of God had come to the daughters of men—an echo from *The Rainbow*. With dubious judgment Lawrence seizes this moment of fulfillment to make an assault on convention. Mellors gives Connie a vulgar accolade when he tells her she is "good cunt," the "best bit of cunt left on earth." The praise seems extravagant and the disquisition on the meaning of the word highly self-conscious.

Again sharp contrast comes into play. The abandon of spring is cruel for Clifford, whose refuge is in formality and order. He believes that the industrial machine is more important than the individual. Connie protests that industry has taken away "natural life and manhood." Clifford views aristocracy not as a matter of blood but as "a function, a part of fate." This intellectual inadequacy is underlined by his physical inadequacy when he insists on going far into the woods, where his electric wheel chair stalls. He is humiliated by having to call Mellors to his assistance but is unconcerned as to whether Mellors might hurt himself in lifting the chair. For the first time Connie hates her husband and berates him for lack of common sympathy. This disgust is capped that evening when in answer to his praise of

Proust, she comments that she is tired of "self-important mentalities."

That evening Connie slips away to the cottage and spends the night with Mellors. For the first time he unburdens himself about his wife and their sexual life. They never met in a simultaneity of passion. From his experience he has concluded that most women want a man, not sex. Most men give in and accept a lie. This he cannot do. For him the right relation with a woman is the very core of life. For a time that evening he is withdrawn and out of sorts. Then they make love on the hearth rug. She admires his penis: "so proud and so lordly." He humorously denominates their respective organs as John Thomas and Lady Jane. They have never been in closer harmony, but he hates it when she asks him if he loves her. The knowledge should come from touch and not from words.

Mellors in his turn assails the ugliness and dehumanization of England. His colonel had said that the middle class were "the mingiest set of ladylike snipe ever invented." As for the working class, "Their spunk is gone dead." He foresees the time when in all races the last real man is killed and men are all tame: the "root of sanity is in the balls," and they are all being emasculated. With such a prospect he thinks it wrong to bring a child into the world. Connie urges him not to say that, since she is going to have his child. Unable to leave because of a sudden rainstorm, she runs naked out into the rain. He throws off his clothing and pursues her, taking her quickly like an animal. He talks to her in "throaty caressive dialect" about her basic animal nature—which makes his real. Then in a symbolic naked marriage they entwine each other's genitals with flowers.

Sir Clifford, armored in egotism, continues to

be unsuspicious. As her pregnancy advances, Connie realizes she must go away from Wragby and arranges a trip to Venice with her father and sister. She spends her last night with Mellors. Hilda and Mellors take an instant dislike to each other. Hilda does not like Connie's lowering herself, though she relents somewhat when she hears Mellors's history. He says Hilda is a stubborn, self-willed woman and he is glad he doesn't have the handling of her. Their night together is one of "reckless, shameless sensuality." They burn out the shames "that can only be eased by sensual fire," "by the phallic hunt of the man."

What we have had up to this point is a return to Eden, to a state of prelapsarian innocence and naturalness. Connie and Mellors have reached this state with some difficulty, but the real difficulties come with the intrusion of the world upon their idyll. To Connie in Venice comes the disturbing news, via Mrs. Bolton, that Mellors's wife has turned up, has tried to move in with her husband, and is spreading scandalous rumors about his entertaining women in his cottage. Sir Clifford has had to discharge him, not crediting, however, a vague rumor about Lady Chatterley. She resolves not to go back to Wragby. Her father, saying that Wragby is more permanent than people's emotions, does not want her to leave her husband. An artist friend, Duncan Forbes, in whom she confides, asserts that society won't let people be straight and open about sex. There is still "one insane taboo left: sex as a natural and vital thing." He is willing to pretend to be the father of the child.

Connie arranges to see Mellors in London. Appropriately their rendezvous is at The Golden Cock on Adam Street. In regular clothes he has a natural distinction, much better than the cut-to-pattern look

of men of Connie's class. The difficult problems the
couple face force Mellors to articulate his creed. He
recognizes that their child represents the future,
which he fears and mistrusts. "If there's got to be a
future for humanity, there'll have to be a very big
change from what now is." The two dare not be together for six months lest they jeopardize the divorce that Mellors is belatedly seeking. Father and
lover meet in a dubious scene in which the father
asks how his daughter is in bed. The two men are
bound, we are told, by the "free-masonry of male
sensuality." Forbes also meets Mellors, who doesn't
like the artist because his pretentious avant-garde
painting is murdering the bowels of human compassion.

Sir Clifford goes completely to pieces when he
learns of his wife's decision to leave him. He becomes almost a child in Mrs. Bolton's hands, "letting go all his manhood and sinking back to a childish position that was really perverse." He holds
Connie to her promise to come back to Wragby for a
time, then is beside himself with rage when he
keeps at her until she confesses that it is Mellors
who is her lover. He categorically refuses to give
her a divorce, even though this means that a
gamekeeper's son will be heir to the baronetcy.

Connie flees from Wragby in desperation. Mellors has gone away to the country to work on a farm
during their enforced separation. The novel ends
with a letter from him in which he expatiates once
more on the decay brought by an industrial society.
If people were taught to *live* instead of to earn and
spend, if the men wore scarlet trousers and danced
and swaggered and were handsome, they could get
along with very little cash. "They ought to learn to
be naked and handsome and to sing in a mass and
dance the old group dances, and carve the stools

they sit on, and embroider their own emblems. Then they wouldn't need money." Mellors sees a bad time coming for the industrial masses. Yet he is hopeful. It is possible to insure against the future only by believing in the best bit of you. So he believes in the little vivifying flame that has leapt between him and Connie. They "fucked a flame into being" just as "the flowers are fucked into being between the sun and the earth." Now that flame must be low and hesitant during their period of waiting. And so, he concludes, "John Thomas says goodnight to Lady Jane, a little droopingly, but with a hopeful heart."

The problem with this novel is less its message than its power to convince. How well does it fulfill the author's dictum in Chapter IX that the novel can lead our sympathies into new places and force "a recoil from things grown dead?" Certainly Lawrence is right to challenge the kind of writing that glorifies "the most corrupt feelings so long as they are conventionally 'pure.' " But I think his challenge comes off much less well than that which Hardy makes in *Tess of the D'Urbervilles*, for example.

The chief weakness of *Lady Chatterley's Lover* is its major characters. They are two-dimensional constructs who are moved about for purposes of demonstration. They never really come alive because they have no depth. This is a pity, for there is a potential for anguish, for struggle with the ineluctability of their condition, in all three of them. Sir Clifford is written off as an insignificant human being right from the start. Connie never quite emerges as a person from the stereotype in which she first appears. Mellors, the most complicated of the three, has his depths unplumbed. The reader really would like to know what goes on inside him, but when Mellors speaks, it is either to instruct Connie about sex or to inveigh against the fallen condition of mankind.

In effect, this work is as much tract as novel. In its protests against the growing mechanization of human beings it uses a wrong attitude toward sex as its main line of argument. It urges that casual sex, indifferent or brutal sex, and cerebral sex be replaced by reverential sex, which is the primal, fertile source of being. Tommy Dukes asserts early in the novel that the only bridge across the chasm between wrong-headed contemporary ways and sane and healthy being is the phallus. This is perhaps a permissible hyperbole, but the verdict is likely to be "not proven." The same reservation applies to the use of four-letter words. Lawrence feels that the words are taboo because society look upon the acts and organs to which they refer as evil and ugly. Unfortunately it does not follow that if we remove the taboos, our attitudes towards sex itself will change. That is a consummation devoutly to be wished for but one not necessarily attained.

Considering all the to-do over *Lady Chatterley's Lover* readers are likely to be astonished at how little space is given over to material that would have been considered objectionable even when the novel came out. The four-letter words are mostly clustered in one short scene. The descriptions of copulation, while numerous, are fairly matter of fact, almost clinical on occasion. They certainly do not inflame desire in the manner of true pornography. Such an effect would be to defeat the purposes of the novel, to destroy the reverential attitude that is its goal. Yet Lawrence himself was ambivalent on the subject of its pornographic effect. He commented that the book must never fall into his mother-in-law's hands, since she would find it too shocking.

Knowing that the novel would never pass muster with a regular publisher, Lawrence arranged to have a thousand copies printed in Florence by a compositor who did not know English. As indicated earlier, the book immediately fell afoul of the law. I suspect Lawrence would have been greatly disappointed if it hadn't. It had an immediate *succès de scandale* and, since it was not covered by copyright, was widely pirated. Lawrence went to Paris in March 1929 to arrange for another privately printed edition to compete with the pirated ones. After his death authorized but abridged editions came out in both London and New York in 1932. It was not until 1960 that the ban was removed in the United States after Grove Press brought out an unexpurgated edition and, when challenged by Post Office officials, won its case in court. Penguin Press had a similar success a few months later. It is reported that the various editions of the novel that came out in 1959 and 1960 have sold over six million copies!

6

•••

The Lesser Novels

The six novels that fall into this category would not be much read today, were it not for the fame of their author. Two of them, *The Trespasser* (1912) and *Kangaroo* (1923), are very bad. Two, *The Lost Girl* (1920) and *Aaron's Rod* (1922), have some interest in that they repeat Lawrence's ideas about love and marriage. And two of them, *The White Peacock* (1911) and *The Plumed Serpent* (1926)—at the beginning and end of the writer's career as novelist— bear the stamp of his originality in quite different ways. With the exception of *The Trespasser* all of them draw heavily on Lawrence's early experiences in the Midlands or on his travel impressions. In one of them, *The Plumed Serpent*, there is present what Lawrence generally lacked, a successful use of novelistic invention.

The White Peacock

This first novel is impressive primarily for its sustained lyricism and for its lack of preaching. In it the writer is content to record the people and the natural phenomena of his native region. The first-person narrator (unique among the novels) is a Lawrence-like figure named Cyril Beardsall. The other princi-

pal characters are his sister Lettie; her fiance and
husband Leslie Tempest, son of a mine owner; and
the Saxton family at Strelley Mill, who clearly de-
rive from Lawrence's friends the Chambers at
Haggs Farm.

Two-thirds of the novel describes what the narrator calls "the bright sea of our youth"—young
people setting out in life very much in the manner
of Tolstoy's young people in *War and Peace*. The
rivalry of Leslie Tempest and George Saxton for
Lettie's hand is the center of the narrative. Lettie's
flirtatiousness is not altogether harmless. She does
lead George on, even while she is becoming conscious that she will ultimately make the conventional worldly choice of Leslie. George on the re-
bound marries his cousin Meg, who runs a pub. The
rest of the Saxton family, unable to make a living at
farming, emigrate to Canada. Cyril leaves for a life
in the south. Other minor characters get married.
The sense of infinite possibility that characterized
their youth is belied by the constrictions of adult
life and subsides into occasional rebellious dreams
of what might have been.

Several fatalities in the early part of the narrative prefigure this later diminished condition. The
Saxton cat, caught in a gamekeeper's trap, is so
badly mangled that it must be destroyed. There is a
pursuit of rabbits that ravage the Saxton farm and of
wild dogs that kill the sheep. Cyril's and Lettie's
father, who had abandoned his family years before,
reappears and ends his life as a derelict, bringing
awareness of happiness missed to his wife and a
wondering compassion in his son. Annable, the
gamekeeper on a neighboring estate who has also
deserted his family and middle-class decorum in
search for personal integrity—a prestudy of Mellors
in *Lady Chatterley's Lover*—is killed in an acci-

dent, leaving his wife and children destitute. These ominous clouds darken the radiant landscape of youth, but are scarcely heeded or understood.

The last third of the novel somewhat sketchily covers the fifteen years following Lettie's and George's marriages as reviewed by Cyril on his occasional visits home. Without domestic ties himself, he is dismayed by the varied states of domestic bondage that he sees among his contemporaries. George Saxton, who has become a drunkard, is despised and ostracized by his wife and children. Lettie, superior to her husband, goes through the routines of wife and mother, but finds little fulfillment in her roles. Cyril hears from his old friend Alice Gall about the boredom of her marriage to sanctimonious Percival Charles. Even the nearly ideal marriage of Emily Saxton to Tom Renshaw, a farmer, strikes Cyril as banal. He is weary of "the young, arrogant, impervious mothers" and their limited horizons. Nothing in these ménages has any permanent attraction for him, and he remains unmarried.

The conclusion of the novel seems almost deliberately anti-Tolstoyan. It questions the exaltation of maternal self-abnegation, as exemplified by Natasha in the second epilogue of *War and Peace* or by Princess Marya in *Family Happiness*. There is no palliation of failures such as that of George Saxton. Not only does the novel not preach a doctrine of self-fulfillment, it is emphatic in its demonstration of unfulfillment in the marriages exhibited. The tone is not one of tortured repudiation of things as they are, but neither is it a Tolstoyan affirmation. What we have, very uncharacteristic of Lawrence, is acceptance of human limits and resignation that that is the way things are.

This work is un-Lawrentian in another respect

as well. Considering its vaguely autobiographical basis, it is remarkably detached. Cyril belongs to a comfortable middle-class level of society; he does not worry about his social status. His mother is a minor character who does not dominate her children. Whatever the sins of the father, the ugliness of family discord is relegated to the past. Cyril's friendships are without tension and without passion. Emily Saxton and he drift apart without acrimony. Cyril is observer only, not active participant in the drama, and therefore not damaged or greatly moved by it.

The Trespasser

Published only a few months after *The White Peacock*, this novel is inferior to its predecessor and completely different from it. It is the only one of Lawrence's novels that may be called dramatic, that is, concentrated in time and action without the ruminative manner characteristic of the author. It is also the only one that is not grounded, at least in part, on daily actuality as Lawrence knew it in a familiar locale. The book is a preliminary attack on cerebral living, but it is rather abstract, arising conceptually from the author's brain rather than sensuously from his experience.

The core of this work is a conventional sexual triangle. Siegmund McNair, a musician of forty, married to Beatrice and father of four children, deserts his family, from whom he has been alienated for some time, to spend five days on the Isle of Wight with Helena, a rather arty, febrile woman. Their idyll, if it be that, consists of a good deal of kissing (consummation does seem to take place at least once in the bracken), a good deal of wandering about on the island, often lost, in a blissful haze, and an inordinate amount of conversation as highfalutin' as the names of the chief characters. The cerebral nature of the affair is underlined by the comment of one of Siegmund's acquaintances that "These deep, interesting women [such as Helena] dont want *us*; they want the flowers of the spirit they can gather of us. We, as natural men, are more or less degrading to them and to their love of us; therefore they destroy the natural man in us—that is, us altogether."

Even though Siegmund is aware of the accuracy of this judgment and is distressed by Helena's passivity and the fact that "her blood runs in bondage, and her kindness is full of cruelty," he cannot reconcile himself to the loss of Helena or the alternative of the limbo to which his family have cast him because of his derelictions. Shortly after his return to London he hangs himself. Helena, drawn back from a vacation in Cornwall by a foreboding of disaster, survives the loss with little emotional damage. While sentimentally attached to the *memory* of Siegmund, in less than a year she is engaging in another cerebral affair with Cecil Byrne.

The issue here is one that becomes increasingly important in Lawrence's later writing: the role of woman as emasculator, therefore as destroyer, and the necessity for a man to escape the nets cast to hem him in. However, the demonstration in this novel is not impressive. None of the three principal characters is fully drawn; they are puppets moved about by authorial fiat, not inner necessity, to a foreordained, and hectic, conclusion.

The Lost Girl

The Lost Girl comes the closest of Lawrence's novels to being a realistic case study. It is unusual also in the disengagement of the author. He is content to depict his milieu, set his characters in motion, and watch what happens to them with minimal commentary or rhetorical underlining.

Alvina Houghton (pronounced Huffton) is a typical product of provincial middle-class environment. She grows up in Woodhouse, a "mining townlet" indistinguishable from Eastwood. It has its social gradations from "the dark of coal-dust" up through the tradesmen and managerial class to "the automobile refulgence" of the colliery manager. Her father, James Houghton, is the proprietor of a draper's shop, stocking goods so far above the taste of his provincial clientele that his business gradually goes broke. His final cast at fortune is to set up in a bad location a theater for movies and vaudeville turns. When he dies at seventy, Alvina is left a hundred pounds or so and some jewels. Even the furniture of the house she has always lived in must go to satisfy her father's creditors. She is the typical, or nearly typical, spinster of the kind that seems to proliferate in such an environment. She has had little chance at marriage, though the advice she receives is to settle for a loveless and conventional union. Instead she trains as a maternity nurse, but then allows herself to be shackled to the needs of her motherless household and to arrive at the age of thirty facing the sterility of spinsterhood.

Nearly half the novel is given over to the impasse in which Alvina finds herself. She does discover a partial, though demeaning, avenue of escape when she undertakes to play the piano at her father's theater. She enjoys her encounters with the troupes of artistes as they pass through on tour. It is one of these troupes that fortuitously gives her life a new direction. The group call themselves Natcha-Kee-Tawara because they present a number of so-called American Indian dance acts. The actors are

in fact Swiss and Italian, and it is the Italian, Cicio—Francesco Morasca—who catches Alvina's
eye. To look into Cicio's yellow eyes is for her "like
meeting a lion." She is enamored of his "dark un-
seizable beauty." She takes an unpaid position with
the troupe and has no hesitation or remorse about
sleeping with Cicio. It is his uncaring peasant solidity that draws her out of her orbit.

The whole Natcha-Kee-Tawara sequence is
tiresome and somewhat silly. It is one of the least
happy of Lawrence's inventions. However, the device serves its purpose by drawing Alvina out of the
sterile, protective shell of her bourgeois values.
With Cicio she learns the loneliness of passion,
which also is "a moment of stillness and completeness." Her break with convention is expressed symbolically when, after her father's death, she and the
young men from the troupe play a game of cards on
Sunday, leading one of her father's associates to exclaim: "You're a lost girl."

Almost penniless when her father's affairs are
settled, she temporarily opts for security and takes a
position as maternity nurse in Lancaster. There she
discovers the satisfaction of having status in the
world, of being a person in her own right. When the
war breaks out she thinks of volunteering, partly to
escape the bondage she foresees in a marriage with
a local doctor, who will not leave her alone. In moments of rebellion she thinks of Natcha-Kee-Tawara. The group has broken up because of the war,
and Cicio suddenly reappears in Alvina's life. She
runs off with him to get married, wondering: "Was it
atavism, this sinking into extinction under the spell
of Cicio?"

The manuscript of the first part of this novel
was left behind in Germany when Lawrence and
Frieda visited England in 1914. The war made it

impossible for the manuscript to be retrieved. Lawrence did not get to revise it until 1919. What he added then is a logical but unexpected graft on the original stalk. There is a detailed and somewhat superfluous account of Alvina's and Cicio's train trip from London to Naples, and then on to the primitive village in the Abruzzi mountains which is his home. This is followed by a harrowing account of the first months spent in the village. Alvina, the comfortably reared English girl, finds herself reduced to a primitive peasant existence. Not only are the physical conditions a reduction to a level of minimal comfort and possessions, but she also sinks in her woman's estate to be the appendage of the male community. Yet she flourishes, gives birth to a healthy child, accepts her subordinate role, and is content to have her being in and for Cicio.

When he is called up (Italy has finally entered the war), she promises to wait for him; he promises to come back. This most unlikely marriage not only gives promises of enduring; it seems to be the making of both partners, who achieve a fullness of being that neither has had before. In a way this work is a prestatement of *Lady Chatterley's Lover*, without the tendentious explicitness of sexual submission and immersion. Here, too, the flowering and contentment of the submissive wife are not particularly convincing. Such conviction as there is rests only on Lawrence's assumptions about the primacy of blood consciousness. If those assumptions are denied— and certainly they are proved neither here nor in *Lady Chatterley*—the beneficent effect of socially unequal unions must remain in doubt.

The virtue of this work is that there is no Lawrence character in it. While it embodies quantities of Lawrentian observation in both the Midlands and Italy, observation that pleases and convinces by its acuity, the action of the novel does not rest directly on the writer's experience. In respect to the faithful rendering of observed actuality it is the most realistic novel that Lawrence wrote. All his characters are ordinary people. Most of them are closely subject to the limitations of their environment and their own nature. The overall course is downhill, with the egregious exception of Alvina and Cicio, both of whom by the beneficent agency of blood consciousness rise out of the mire of mediocrity in which they seem doomed to sink. Lawrence is anti-determinist, but here he mutes the affirmation of the ending. Conscious of the uncertainties awaiting Cicio in the war and the uncertain status of Alvina alone in an alien and hostile community, the reader can only hope.

It is this basically mediocre work that brought Lawrence the one evidence of establishment approval that he received in his lifetime. In December 1921 the James Tait Black memorial prize was awarded him. It was worth £100, the most money the author had seen in some time.

Aaron's Rod

Eliseo Vivas in his *The Failure and the Triumph of Art* lists this novel among Lawrence's failures. It is certainly a most imperfect artifact, an imperfection that is no doubt highlighted by the fact that here the novelist has begun to cross the line between fiction and special pleading.[1]

As in *The Trespasser*, the protagonist is a man seeking escape from domestic discord and bondage. Again the scene, initially, is a Midlands mining village. Aaron Sisson, thirty-three, a check-weighman in a mine and also a flautist of professional caliber,

has at the center of his being "a hard core of irratio-
nal, exhausting withholding of himself." He is re-
sistant to the emotional demands of his family; he
refuses to be forced into caring when care is not in
him. Accordingly, having made financial provision
for his wife and children, he deserts them and sets
out on a quest for true independence. His rather
desultory movement toward that goal constitutes
the framework of the narrative. For a time he plays
the flute in a London orchestra. Then he sets out for
Italy, where in Florence he finds an ambience more
nurturing of male well-being. His moral health and
his music flower for a time—hence Aaron's rod.
Then the flute is destroyed when a bomb bursts in a
café about the same time that Aaron wearies of an
affair with an Italian marchesa. It is not clear how
the phallic pun implicit in the title *Aaron's Rod* re-
lates to this double loss.

There are a number of strands of ideas that the
novel carries along rather casually. One is the emptiness and hypocrisy of upper-class life. At the beginning of the novel, as a gesture of resistance
against his family's demands Aaron spends
Christmas Eve getting drunk at the home of one of
the mine owners, whose family and friends lead
vacuous if not vicious lives. He renews acquaintance with the group when he is playing in London
and is further depressed by the emptiness of their
existence. The only one among them who interests
Aaron is Rawdon Lilly, a writer, who is caustic in his
refusal of the values of the group. Aaron's attack on
philistinism continues somewhat unfairly when,
presenting a letter of introduction, he stays with Sir
William Franks in Novara in Italy. The reception
goes far beyond the demands of courtesy, but the
guest is unsparing of his hosts. Finally in Florence
Aaron consorts with another arty, shallow group, in

particular two rich dilettantes who take up and drop
Aaron with a casual condescension that exacerbates
his lower-class sensitivity. All these encounters, including the liaison with a marchesa, serve as a
warning to Aaron not to sacrifice his integrity to the
shallow forms of middle- and upper-class society.

This shallowness is equated in part with a general postwar breakdown, though it would seem to
be of longer standing than that. Lilly, who has
passed through Socialism, has reached the conclusion that "people are not *men*! They are insects and
instruments, and their destiny is slavery." His object
is to get out of "this miserable heap," out of "all that
mass-consciousness, all that mass activity." But alas,
the narrative voice concludes, "the verbal and the
ostensible, the accursed mechanical ideal gains day
by day over the spontaneous life-dynamic."

These discontents are, however, only incidental background to the main thrust of the novel.
Aaron and Lilly are both Lawrence-figures, a super-
erogation that nonetheless makes for an interesting
formal pattern. Their courses are parallel, Lilly the
mentor to direct the uncertain steps of Aaron, a
Vergil to Aaron's Dante. Lilly hates married people
"who are two in one—stuck together like two jujube
lozenges." He sees women and their children as
agents of tyranny. He resents the fact that his wife
resists him, feeling that she should somewhere be
submissive. He seeks, and imagines he finds, a better human relationship among the primitives, the
Aztecs and the Red Indians, for example—about
whom in fact he knows nothing—because they have
"living pride," unlike the "flea-bitten Asiatics."
"Even Niggers are better than Asiatics."

Aaron, also seeking male integrity, rejoices in
Florence, where the sight of the male statues in
front of the Signoria "seemed to start a new man in

him." It is his conviction that in love, or sex, "the man should be the asker and the woman the answerer." In contemporary society those roles are reversed and he does not see how a man "with one drop of real spunk can stand it long." He resists and rejects woman's "terrible will, like a flat cold snake coiled round his soul and squeezing him to death."

Lilly, bitten by a desire for leadership, has as his first principle that there is no god outside of man, "who can't even gum himself to a divine Nirvana moon." A man cannot resign initiative to a higher power. He must not deny the Holy Spirit, which is within him. He must not deny his responsibility by "loving or sacrificing or Nirvanaing—or even anarchising and throwing bombs." Lilly tells Aaron that men must find and submit to a greater soul in a man or a woman, must submit to "the positive power-soul in man, for their being." When Aaron, puzzled, asks: "Whom shall I submit to?", the answer is irritatingly vague: "Your soul will tell you." At that uncertain point the novel ends.

This novel affords good evidence of the inadequacy of Lawrence's thinking when it came to problems of leadership. Dissatisfaction with the state of society leads to arrogant racism and an uncritical exaltation of the primitive. None of this is really experiential. It is all wishful thinking, and the inescapable inference that Lawrence was thinking of himself as an acceptable and accepted leader of men is risible.

Kangaroo

Kangaroo is a genuinely perfunctory performance. As an examination of what ails the world it is interesting. As an evocation of the physical and human

landscape of Australia it is perhaps the most exten-
sive and sensitive of Lawrence's travel impressions.
As a novel it does not get off the ground.

On their voyage eastward to San Francisco in
1922 the Lawrences spent a period of less than six
months in Australia, a good part of the time in relative isolation in a beach cottage south of Sydney.
The rawness and strangeness of the continent made
a strong impression on them. Lawrence was fascinated by the power of the Pacific as it beat upon the
shore near their cottage. He was exhilarated—but
alternately depressed—by the process of becoming,
the unfinished state, of this new land. Gradually, if
we are to trust the novel, he came to hate and fear
Australia, as he did all non-European landscapes
even when he was repudiating things European.
He may have offended Australian pride, but it is
true that he rendered the strangeness and the empty
vastness of the country with remarkable exactness
and sensitivity.

It is this newness, strangeness, and potential
promise that trigger the speculative content of *Kangaroo*, a speculation about the kind of leadership
the country needs. This ideological content is minimally supported by narrative action. Two Euro-
peans, Richard Lovat Somers, a writer, and his wife,
Harriet—characters identical in all important respects to the Lawrences—visit Australia for a few
months, encounter remarkably few of its citizens,
are drawn to and then repelled by the representa-
tives of two contending political factions, and ultimately disengage themselves from both and from
concern for Australia's future. The people whom
they encounter are in part well drawn. Jack and Vic-
toria Callcott have vivid and vulgar provincial personalities. Jaz Trewhella comes through less suc-
cessfully. Struthers, the socialist leader, and

Benjamin Cooley—"Kangaroo"—the leader of a
protofascist movement, are monolithic embodi-
ments of doctrine with little human substance.

Most of the trouble with this novel is that nothing happens except for the attraction-repulsion
movement of Somers toward and away from the two
ideologies. This dramatic movement within
Somers's mind is rather embryonically paralleled
by a conflict also within Somers between his innate
nature of isolate and the demands of solidarity that
any attempt at leadership will entail. But neither internal struggle reaches a point of heightened conflict or carries the reader along. Rather Somers
never seems of more significance than a stray in-
truder who for a time entertains himself by dipping
a toe in the political waves, but whom no commitment will prevent from going away when he is tired
of the game. He has arrived as a tourist and he departs as a tourist, perhaps to reenact a similar pseu-
doinvolvement somewhere else.

The clumsiest thing about this novel is its
abundant undigested materials. Almost exactly one-
fifth of the text is given over to a detailed and extraneous account of the humiliations and persecution
suffered by the Somers in Cornwall during World
War I. This account is supposed to explain Somers'
alienation. Yet cause and effect seem largely uncon-
nected. At any rate placing this material in the novel
throws the whole work out of balance. The reader
carries away the uncomfortable feeling that Lawrence is padding the novel and venting his spleen
some six or seven years after the event—for the experiences are his and Frieda's without any distillation or alteration.

To recapitulate, Australia, a *tabula rasa*, an
empty space demanding the creation of a new way
of life, triggers in Somers, a man who is deeply

alienated from outworn European forms and who has physically run away from them, an examination of possible new ways of social organization. This examination at the same time sets off within him a self-examination to determine what his part in such a renovation should or could be. Thus, if this novel were less chaotic, there could be a double outcome: a recognition that the competing ideologies are inadequate or false or both, and that the aspirations of the man tempted to leadership are impossible because of the limitations of his own nature.

The Plumed Serpent

This is the most imaginative, the most powerful, and the most misunderstood of Lawrence's novels. It is no doubt also a failure, but it is not an ignominious failure like *Kangaroo*, and it does have an important place in the arch of the writer's aspiration. It is the closest he comes to setting forth an embodiment of an ideal human condition, of the wholeness of being and attunement with natural forces by which he was long obsessed.

The scene is Mexico, a Mexico simplified and symbolized for the purposes of the novel. It has the stark simplicity and garish colors of an Orozco mural. There is no literal correspondence with the country Lawrence visited in 1923 and again in the winter of 1924–25. Undoubtedly his representation draws heavily also on his impressions of New Mexico, where he spent a much longer time. Carleton Beals, an American ambassador to Mexico, finds *The Plumed Serpent* to be "a remarkably intuitive book," though he thinks Lawrence never understood Mexico and was frightened of it.[2] Witter Bynner, who was with him much of the time in Mexico,

calls the first half of the novel "a consummate piece
of noticing and writing," but scoffs at the second
part.[3] Intuitive or not, well observed or not, basically the Mexico of this novel is a construct, a
mythological setting populated by sullen earth-
bound figures struggling for a potency to match that
of the pulsing earth and the radiant sky.

It is readily apparent that the three principal
characters never come alive. Individual being is
again subordinate to symbolic function. Kate Leslie,
twice widowed, in middle age restless and unsatisfied, undergoes the culture shock of Mexico, resists
it, succumbs to it, and, to the extent that she can
allow it, is made whole by immersion in it. Her experience is shaped by Don Ramón Carrasco and
General Cipriano Viedma, who are leading a movement that will be the transformation of the inchoate
mass of their countrymen.

The novel opens with satiric "Wasteland" incidents, first of a bullfight, then of a banal tea party
where American residents exhibit their stereotyped
incomprehension of Mexico. Kate Leslie can stand
neither experience. Nor does she respond favorably
to the frenetic life of Mexico City and the "great un-
der-drift of squalor and heavy reptile-like evil" that
she feels all around her. She thinks that the famous
Rivera murals are a shout of hatred. In the eyes of
both men and women she discerns an "uncreated
centre, where the evil and insolence lurked." She
feels that America is "the great death-continent,"
and that "Viva la muerte" is its motto. Even as she
resists, she feels that Mexico pulls her down, perhaps beneficially as the earth pulls one down so
that he can balance on his feet and "send roots into
the dark places again."

The charisma of Don Ramón Carrasco out-
weighs the revulsion that impels Kate to flee from

Mexico. She temporizes by leaving Mexico City and taking a house on the shore of Lake Sayula, a lake that belongs to the old gods of Mexico. She is fascinated and repelled by her stay there: "There is something rich and alive in these people. They want to be able to breathe the Great Breath." It is at the lake that she first becomes aware of the rise of the Morning Star, a new religion that seeks to bring back the old Indian deity Quetzalcoatl. This is a movement of men, but Kate is permitted to join them in a ritual dance and feels herself caught up in "the slowly revolving ocean of nascent life," as her desires, her individuality, her will merge "in the ocean of the great desire."

From this point on the two major actions of the novel are interrelated. One is the rebirth of Mexico under the aegis of the Morning Star movement. The other is the regeneration of Kate Leslie through participation in that movement. Both are tied symbolically to the greening power of water, to a baptism of the individual, to cleansing rains that bring fertility to the wasteland of the old order.

The radical renovating power of the Morning Star movement must compete with the entrenched, self-seeking power of both the Roman Catholic church and the Mexican socialist revolution. The leaders of the movement try to conciliate these two opponents, or at least to soften their opposition. Don Ramón is scornful of the goals of the socialist government: "Politics, and all this *social* religion that Montes [the president of Mexico] has got is like washing the outside of the egg, to make it look clean. But I, myself, I want to go into the egg, right to the middle, to start it growing into a new bird." Ramón also fails in his conversations with the bishop; his plea for a truly catholic church in which each race would worship in terms of its own blood and its own ancient beliefs falls on deaf ears. Indeed within his own family a chasm opens up over religion. His wife, Doña Carlota, flees from Don Ramón as from the devil, taking their children with her.

As the movement gathers momentum, its purposes are underlined by a series of hymns chanted by the initiate and later by the people. The first of these hymns—repetitive free-verse chants—herald the return of the ancient Mexican gods. The fourth hymn is bitter against foreigners for diverting and debasing the current of Mexican attunement with the universe. The culmination is reached one Sunday when to the chanting of a hymn in farewell to Jesus, whom the great God has called home, the townspeople empty the church of Christian images. These are taken across the lake to an island, where they are burned as the sky clouds up for thunder and rain.

The covert warfare between upholders of the old and proponents of the new comes into the open with an attempt on Don Ramón's life. Seven men are killed and he is seriously wounded before Kate Leslie's help saves him from death. The Morning Star rapidly gathers strength after this. The once inert peons shake off their submissiveness to church and foreigner, and begin to feel life again. The church at Sayula is reopened as the church of Quetzalcoatl, with its own ritual and its own images. (Don Ramón's wife Carlota creeps in and dies of convulsions because of the sacrilege she witnesses.) A second deity, Huitzilopochtli, comes to the fore. He is the avenger, the destroyer, red as blood. General Cipriano Viedma represents him and creates an army to do his service. The first act of the second god is to punish those responsible for Don Ramón's near assassination. After appropriate ceremony two of the leaders of the conspiracy are garroted. Three of the four others are stabbed to death by Cipriano. The living Quetzalcoatl and the living Huitzilopochtli join each other in the church in evidence of their oneness of being and purpose.

The movement now sweeps everything before it. The president makes the religion of Quetzalcoatl the national religion. The churches of the old religion are closed. The armies of Huitzilopochtli and the priesthood of Quetzalcoatl appear in all the towns and villages. "The whole country was thrilling with a new thing, with a release of new energy. But there was a sense of violence and crudity in it all, a touch of horror."

Kate Leslie after some hesitation marries General Viedma and takes her place in the living pantheon as Malintzi, the consort of Huitzilopochtli. She is happy to realize that "Alone she was nothing. Only as the pure female corresponding to his pure male, did she signify." She welcomes Cipriano because he has "the ancient phallic mystery, the ancient god-devil of the male Pan." She feels "the leap of the old, antediluvian blood-male into union with her. And for this, without her knowing, her innermost blood had been thudding all the time." For the first time in her life Kate feels "absolutely at rest." "What she had; with Cipriano was curiously beyond her knowing; so deep and hot and flowing, as it were subterranean . . ." "She lived in his aura, and he, she knew, lived in hers, with nothing said, and no personal or spiritual intimacy whatever. A mindless communion of the blood." Even so, Kate is not completely reconciled to this submission. She keeps thinking of a return to Europe, but recognizes this would be a renegade act, a turning back from her true well-being. Thus it is that, at the end of the novel, she begs Cipriano not to let her go away.

Most readers will find the insistence on blood consciousness as the way to total personal and communal well-being overstated and irritatingly vague. And some see it as dangerously like the doctrine preached and practiced by the Nazis in Germany in the 1930s. It seems to me that the virtue of *The Plumed Serpent* is that it does not completely underwrite the formula that it presents with such thunderous rhetoric. There is violence, crudity, and horror in the movement, and for Kate the submission that involvement with Cipriano entails is not acceptable on the level of reason. What I am suggesting is that the whole novel is a speculation about what kind of total belief might bring a dead society to life, a speculation carefully based on the primitive psychic springs of Mexican life, but that the presentation is not prescriptive, does not say: Thus it should be.

7

●●

Short Stories
and Novellas

During the twenty years of his active writing career
Lawrence produced over fifty short stories and
seven short novels. The distinction between these
two forms is in fact rather blurred. "Daughters of
the Vicar" and "The Princess" might easily be in-
cluded among the short novels, and *Love among
the Haystacks* is more properly a short story. Lawrence himself seems to have had no feeling about
the separation of the two forms.

The first collection of his prose fiction, *The
Prussian Officer and Other Stories*, was published
in 1914. It contained three stories earlier presented
in *The English Reveiw*. *England, My England and
Other Stories* came out in 1922, and a third collection, *The Woman Who Rode Away and Other Stories*, in 1928. Other collections appeared soon after
Lawrence's death, and in 1961 forty-seven of the
short stories were brought out in the three-volume
Viking and Penguin editions. It is from these volumes and from the two-volume *Short Novels* (1956)
that most readers today come to know Lawrence's
short prose fiction.

These pieces have a considerable range of subject and setting, though in the last analysis a substantial majority deal with sexual tension, or occa-
sionally sexual comedy. It is not possible to detect

any development in skill in handling these forms. Some of the most powerful stories appear in the first volume. Such change as there is is a movement away from the basically dramatic treatment of the earlier stories to something resembling parable in a number of the later ones, and a shift from a relatively neutral narrative stance to one of forceful partisanship, on occasion approaching outright invective. Many of the stories are run of the mill productions, but enough of them exhibit Lawrence's most concentrated power to qualify them as the best part of his oeuvre. One obvious reason for such a judgment is that the short forms discourage the writer's penchant for repetitive statement and his tendency to preach.

As we might expect, it is the early stories that make use of the Eastwood background. "Strike-Pay," "A Sick Collier," "Her Turn," "Tickets, Please" are unpretentious studies of life in a mining community. The outstanding piece in this group is the often-anthologized "Odour of Chrysanthemums," the first story by Lawrence published in *The English Review* (1911). It is without flaw—nothing superfluous, nothing tendentious. The opening paragraph evokes the drab hopelessness of the region. It is autumn. In Elizabeth Bates's garden are "ragged wisps" of pink chrysanthemums, which give the harried miner's wife fugitive spiritual sustenance. Her situation closely resembles that of Mrs. Morel in *Sons and Lovers*. Wife and children await the coming home of Walter Bates, who is given to drink and is likely to loiter at the pub while his supper gets cold. His wife's smoldering anger turns to alarm as the hours pass and she listens to the senile maunderings of Walter's mother, who is also alarmed. None of the neighbors has seen him since work. Finally his mates go to look for him and find him dead of asphyxiation in the mine.

They bring his body back to the cottage, knocking over a vase of chrysanthemums as they lay him in the cold, unused parlor. His mother jealously joins his wife in the ritual of laying out, to the deathly smell of the spilled flowers. The wife, contemplating the body of her dead husband, realizes that they have lived together as strangers: "There had been nothing between them, and yet they had come together, exchanging their nakedness repeatedly." "They had met in the dark and had fought in the dark, not knowing whom they met nor whom they fought." Mrs. Bates's heart bursts with pity and grief because "she had refused him as himself." In grief she recognizes what she had also known in anger, that their relationship had been hopeless long before he died. That part of her life is closed. Whatever the difficulties ahead, she knows that she must give herself to life, "her immediate master," at the same time as she draws back in fear and shame from death, "her ultimate master." The story is low-keyed, clear-sighted in its recognition of the barriers to human happiness. It is the most compassionate statement Lawrence ever made.

A quite different statement emerges from "Daughters of the Vicar," which deals with the problem of safety in marriage, particularly as it is conditioned by class consciousness. Here anguish comes from denial of the vital forces of life because of artificial attitudes. Again the scene is a mining community, where a new vicar and his wife try to maintain their assumed superior status on one hundred and twenty pounds a year. The miners ignore them, and they have no standing among the "common vulgar tradespeople." Their children, born

with appalling regularity, grow up emotionally
starved in the frustrated household. The two older
daughters, Mary and Louisa, taught to scorn avail-
able suitors, seem destined for spinsterhood and
servitude to their self-absorbed parents. Mary takes
advantage of a dubious opportunity offered by her
father's temporary assistant, Mr. Massy. Not only is
he no more physically developed than a boy of
twelve, but he lacks "the full range of human feelings." In spite of his arrogance, his physical unat-
tractiveness, his encasement in his sterile life of
logic, Mary convinces herself that the man does not
matter so long as there is a prospect of pecuniary
ease. In such a bargain "The man was a trifle
thrown in." However, she soon comes to sense
vaguely that "she was murdering herself."

If this is safety, Louisa will have none of it; she
would rather be safe in a workhouse. When the
Massy family come to the vicarage for a Christmas
visit, she seeks escape by going to see a Mrs. Durant, a small shopkeeper, whom she finds lying half-
paralyzed in her garden. Louisa promptly takes over
the care of Mrs. Durant and her son Alfred, a collier,
even washing the latter's back when he comes
home from the mine. In spite of his vulgar origins,
the lowliness of his occupation, and the bad reputation of his brothers, Louisa is physically attracted to
him. Her family humiliate him when he comes to
dinner, but the marriage goes through. Her family,
in their stiff-necked pride, think it is a very good
idea when the young couple decide to emigrate to
Canada and remove themselves as a source of em-
barrassment.

A third area explored in this early volume is
that of physical and psychological violence, a surprising interest on the part of sensitive Lawrence.
The two stories that embody this are "The Thorn in

the Flesh" and "The Prussian Officer," both by implication antimilitarist. The former is a simple account of a German soldier on maneuvers in Alsace who is crushed by the military machine. The latter tells of a duel, covertly homosexual in origin, in which a German captain, obscurely drawn to the forthright manliness of his orderly, persecutes the youth to such a degree that the latter murders the officer. After the murder the soldier's anguish leads to a night of hallucination in the forest and then to his death.

The 1922 volume of stories concentrates on sexual tension, especially as one partner attempts to coerce the other. "Samson and Delilah" and "Wintry Peacock" are comic in effect. "You Touched Me" suggests the theme of the novella, "The Fox," as a young man of uncertain origins brings a woman of gentler nurture to marriage. In "Monkey Nuts" a British soldier resists the overtures of an auxiliary-service girl of superior class. The situation is reversed in "Fanny and Annie," where a girl accepts the humiliations of a lower-class marriage. In "The Horse-Dealer's Daughter" we see the poignant situation of a young woman left destitute when her male-centered family falls apart. With almost blind instinct she seeks out the local doctor, who, to his surprise, finds himself accepting her offer of marriage.

The title story of *England, My England* is by far the most probing in this group. It develops a favorite Lawrence subject, the emasculation of the male by the female partner. Winifred and Egbert, married and very much in love, depend heavily on her father's financial support. It is to her father that she refers if she is in difficulty. After the birth of their children there is almost total dependence on her father. Egbert is gradually nudged aside. Winifred's

physical passion for him becomes of secondary importance. She even resents the sexual hold he has
on her and despises him for his, to her, feckless
ways. He stands for nothing, he does not come to
grips with life. He does not feel much in common
with a society that has become overelaborated. Yet,
to his wife's annoyance, Egbert does try to pull his
weight in the rearing of the children. She has to accept the fact that he is not a complete nonentity. Almost providentially the eldest child suffers a knee
injury that necessitates her residence in London for
treatment. There is no room for Egbert there.

When World War I breaks out, he resists the
pressures of mass emotion. He simply ignores the
public issues in the interest of his own independence of spirit. But in time he does start thinking of
joining up, much as he hates the idea of putting
himself in the power of his inferiors. Upon his fa-
ther-in-law's advice he does enlist—but as a common soldier. Thereafter his wife's attitude alters.
She feels it her patriotic duty physically to serve the
soldier, but she repudiates the man. It is a relief to
both of them when he is sent off to the Flanders
front. He is killed by a German shell, and in the
moment of dissolution he is not sustained by any
"straws of life from the past." He prefers dissolving
into the black sea of death, "to any reaching back
towards life." The irony of the story is in the title.
Egbert is no Rupert Brooke. He has not died for
England, or for his wife and children, or for anything. He has just given up. Yet the implication is
that there should have been commitment. In a society whose forms are perhaps sterile, even crum-
bling, the one thing that sustains is a constructive
exercise of will. Still such a statement is ambiguous:
perhaps such exercise of will is impossible.

The stories from the last five years of

Lawrence's life (most of them appearing in *The Woman Who Rode Away*, 1928, or in the posthumous *The Lovely Lady*, 1933) show a heightened misogyny, a movement from the dramatic to the parable, and a renewed fascination with violence. Two stories, "The Lovely Lady" and "Mother and Daughter," are good examples of misogyny. The lovely lady of the story is a domineering mother of seventy-two who holds her son's and niece's lives in suspension while she draws sustenance from them. The niece unmasks her, making her son exclaim: "Why, mother, you're a little old lady!" Once the façade is pierced, the old woman goes to pieces and soon dies. The son realizes that she had no love, not even for herself, and that it was power to feed on other lives that had kept her going. Even in death she has hit out against her son and niece by leaving the bulk of her wealth to a museum.

In "Mother and Daughter" another lovely lady has smothered the life of her daughter, who eventually accepts the suit of a sixty-year-old Armenian merchant. The mother is disgusted, pitying her daughter for being the harem type after all. The pity is reciprocated: "All the harem was left out of you, so perhaps it had to be put back in me" is the daughter's judgment.

Lawrence's several ventures into the occult do not come off. Katherine Mansfield, who published "The Shadow in the Rose Garden," said it was the poorest story he wrote but still better than what others were doing. "The Border Line" is no doubt his most successful venture in this vein. In it a woman, who has remarried after her soldier husband's death in World War I, realizes the male inadequacy of her new husband when, in Strasbourg, she encounters the spirit of her first husband and "moves into the aura of the man to whom she belongs." She is belatedly aware of the "intangible soft flood of contentment" experienced with a husband that is a woman's "perfection and her highest attainment." In the ashes of the postwar world her first husband has come back to save her. When she is met by her living husband in Germany, she sees that his strength is in his weakness, in his clinging dependence, and she despises him. He falls ill, and she solaces herself with the ghost of her first husband as the second lies dead in the other bed in the hotel room. This treatment of the unconscious has reasonable power and credibility. "Glad Ghosts," on the other hand, succeeds in being nothing more than fantasy. "The Rocking Horse Winner" is so completely fantasy as to be amusing and acceptable.

It is the return to psychosexual violence that is most notable in these last stories, particularly in "The Princess" and "The Woman Who Rode Away," both of which have a setting in the American Southwest. Henrietta Urquhart, a motherless child, has been brought up by her father very much as a princess, oddly self-sufficient and as impervious as crystal. She is the embodiment of perfect, sterile virginity. Her very look can enrage coarse males to whom "the phallic mystery was the only mystery." She receives a considerable fortune from her mother's family on condition that she spend half the year in the United States. When her father dies, she is thirty-eight, still a perfect unchanging artifact, "a scentless flower." Though she has thought of marriage in the abstract as an experience she should have, she is untouched by sexual desire. The necessary man too remains an abstraction.

The Princess and her equally virginal companion, Miss Cummins, go to the Rancho del Cerro Gordo for a change of scene. There she has many would-be suitors, who are speedily put off by her impervious manner. The only man who interests her is Domingo Romero, one of the guides, the peasant descendant of what had once been a distinguished family. He is a stoic Mexican of the type that seems either to be waiting to die or to be aroused into magnificent passion. A quiet, reserved intimacy grows up between him and the Princess, though she cannot allow herself to think of him as an adjunct to her desire for marriage. She determines, however, not to leave the ranch until Romero has taken her deep into the mountains where she can see the wild animals. With Miss Cummins as chaperone they will pack in to a mountain cabin that belongs to him.

When Miss Cummins's horse is injured in a fall, the Princess stubbornly goes on alone with Romero. There is an encounter with Indians that is somehow ominous. The mountains are grim and repellent, inhuman and antilife. For the first time in her life the Princess is frightened, wanting to go back, yet forcing herself to go on. The cabin is little more than a shelter, where both must sleep, she in the bed, he on the floor. During the night she awakens with cold, needing warmth and protection, needing to be taken away from herself. She wakes up Romero, who undertakes to keep her warm. She hates the ensuing sexual experience, the mauling and the physical domination, and the pride and joy that surge up in him at her expense. Next day when she wants to leave, he is resentful, especially when she admits that she did not like sex with him. He is determined to make her like it, throwing her clothing and saddle into a pool and holding her prisoner until she will give in to him and willingly accept his domination. When on the fourth day two forest rangers appear, Romero shoots at them and is shot and killed. The Princess takes refuge in fantasy that conceals the facts of the situation and leaves for the East. "Later she married an elderly man, and seemed pleased."

A wife, who discovers in her thirties that her being is unfulfilled, is the protagonist of "The Woman Who Rode Away." She had stopped conscious development at marriage. Her husband meant nothing to her physically, but morally he kept her "in invincible slavery." After years of living in isolation in northern Mexico she is overcome "by a foolish romanticism" that leads her to wonder about "the mysterious, marvellous Indians of the mountains." She sets out alone on horseback and meets some Indians who take her to a sequestered valley. There she tells the chief medicine man that she seeks the gods of the Chilchui Indians because she is weary of her own god.

She is received with inordinate ceremony and attentions that she cannot understand. She is dressed in Indian garments and kept prisoner in a special house. She never sees a woman but is tended and contemplated by men, who treat her with a nonsexual, impersonal solicitude. She witnesses a tribal dance ritual that makes her feel that womanhood as she has experienced it, "intensely personal and individual, was to be obliterated again, and the great primeval symbols were to tower once more over the fallen individual independence of woman." Her Indian mentor tells her that white people know nothing and that the Indian gods will take over the world again when a white woman is sacrificed to them. Obviously she is being prepared for that sacrifice. She surrenders self completely and goes "into that other state of passional cosmic consciousness." With great ceremony she is led to a cave on a rocky promontory where, stretched naked on a stone, she awaits the knife at the moment the sun goes down. Thus the tribe will fulfill prophecy and achieve the power that men must hold for mastery, a power that passes from race to race.

The seven novellas—short novels so called in the two-volume Heinemann edition—are mostly from the middle period, in which, having finished the major novels, Lawrence showed his power in the shorter form. Three of these, *The Fox, The Captain's Doll*, and *St. Mawr*, are considered by many to be the high point of Lawrence's writing.

The other four short novels are worth quick attention. *Love among the Haystacks* (written 1913–14 but published posthumously) is a genial rustic comedy. Two brothers, contrasted in temperament but rivals for the experience of love, both achieve it one night during the harvest when they are guarding the haystacks. *The Ladybird* (what we call a ladybug) is a rather labored contrast between the Dionysian and the disciplined elements in individuals, with a glance at fundamental changes in European society brought about by World War I. *The Virgin and the Gipsy* is interesting chiefly for its cataclysmic ending. The situation is something of a Lawrence stereotype. The vicarage at Papplewick is tyrannically ruled by the vicar's mother, the most ferociously egotistic of all Lawrence's dowagers. The vicar's two daughters are being atrophied in this life-denying atmosphere, which has already dried up their Aunt Cissie. The younger and still adventurous daughter Yvette encounters a gipsy peddler, whose band is encamped in the neighborhood. She envies his freedom and unconventionality and feels an unseemly sexual attraction. The gipsy reports to her that the fortuneteller in his band has said that Yvette must be braver in her body and must listen for the voice of water. She is not brave enough to go to say goodbye to him as she has promised, but he comes to her providentially just after a dam breaks and its waters, sweeping down on the village, engulf the vicarage and drown the grandmother. He saves Yvette from drowning by carrying her to an upper room, where they strip off their sodden clothing and save themselves from hypothermia by huddling naked together during the night that follows. The gipsy tactfully departs before she awakes. The prophecy is fulfilled. Yvette has been liberated from the tyranny of her grandmother and has, inferentially, experienced liberation of the flesh.

The remaining novella, *The Man Who Died*, is a companion piece to *Lady Chatterley's Lover* in its deliberate challenge of convention and in a certain lack of taste. Its original title, *The Escaped Cock*, under which it was first published in Paris in 1929, is an obvious phallic pun, and the introductory portion of the story about the Galilean peasant whose brave and handsome rooster escapes confinement is irrelevant to the narrative proper. Lawrence gives a concise description of the story as one in which "after the Crucifixion Jesus gets up and feels very sick about everything and can't stand the old crowd anymore—so cuts out—and as he heals up, he begins to find what an astonishing place the phenomenal world is, far more marvellous than any salvation or heaven—and thanks his stars he needn't have a 'mission' anymore."

After leaving the hut of the peasant who found him, Jesus' wanderings take him to a temple of Isis on the Mediterranean shore. There fortuitously both he and the priestess witness the first clumsy coupling of two young slaves. The priestess permits him to take refuge in the temple precincts, convinced he is the lost Osiris. In the temple at night they come together. She anoints the scars from the crucifixion, gradually making him whole and aware of the fullness of life. Jesus concludes that the woman is the rock on which he builds his life and that his resurrection is his newly arisen sexual vitality. When the priestess is with child by him, he knows he must leave before those around her betray him to the Roman authorities. They will not meet again, but she has truly brought him back to life.

Of the three remaining novellas only *St. Mawr* is flawed—and that not fatally—by preaching. *The Fox*, which is the earliest of the three, is set in rural England during World War I. Two young women, referred to only by their surnames as March and Banford, have taken over Bailey Farm, intending to make a living by raising chickens. They are floored by the hard work, by the disasters common to poultry raising, and by the wartime scarcities. They are particularly enraged by the bold depredations of a fox. One evening March actually sees the animal, who looks at her "half inviting, half contemptuous and cunning," so that thereafter he comes somehow to dominate her unconscious, putting her under a kind of spell.

The narrative is reticent about what has drawn the two women together. The mannishness of March and the delicate fragility of Banford suggest a lesbian relationship, a bringing together of complementary natures in what appears to be a durable union. Into this domestic setting comes a young soldier on leave, Henry Grenfel, who had once lived on this farm with his grandfather. March immediately identifies him with the fox, an analogy that the reader finds acceptable as he sees the young man insinuate himself into the household, while maintaining a kind of sly self-sufficiency in his night prowlings. He is not consciously predatory, but he does look to his own comfort, and soon the idea comes to him that beneath March's mannish exterior there is a woman whom he wants as wife. One night as he prowls around the place, he kills the fox, a way of saying that he has become the fox.

A quiet tug of war develops between Henry and Banford for March. Banford warns her friend that marriage will mean that she will be "bossed and bullied by a hateful, red-faced boy, a beastly labourer." March dreams that night that Banford is dead and laid in her coffin with the fox's fur over her. A few days later March appears at tea in a dress, for the first time letting Henry see her feminine softness. She concedes that she cannot see herself and Banford as two old women together and hesitantly agrees to get married at Christmas. However, once Henry has gone back to his regiment, March writes to him calling off the marriage. He gets emergency leave and cycles sixty miles back to the farm, arriving just as the two women are clumsily trying to fell a Scotch fir. As he turns to and helps them, he has a kind of wishful foreknowledge that the tree will fall on Banford. It does, and he knows he has won.

Still, after their marriage he does not possess March completely. She has found it hard to "accept the submergence which his new love put upon her," in contrast to the authority, the responsibility of her relation with Banford. Sometimes Henry regrets what he has done, wishing he had left the two women to kill each other. He is impatient to take his wife away to Canada, where he hopes she will give in to him, where "he would have all his own life as a young man and a male, and she would have all her own life as a woman and a female."

The Captain's Doll represents a more complicated and sophisticated relationship. Alexander Hepburn, a captain in the British occupation forces in Germany, has Countess Hannele as his mistress. She is a skilled maker of dolls, and the one she makes of the captain in his tight tartan trews is a masterpiece. Word gets to the captain's wife in England that something is going on. She promptly appears in Germany, becomes acquainted with the countess, and mistakenly concludes that it is Hannele's friend and business partner who is Hepburn's lover. Mrs. Hepburn also is determined to buy the doll. The skill with which she extends her power over her husband and the enjoyment with which she manipulates him provide a marvelous satiric portrait of this self-centered, shallow, unscrupulous woman.

Under circumstances that are not clear Mrs. Hepburn falls out of a window and is killed. The captain, at last free, retires from the army and leaves Germany, losing touch with Hannele. After a considerable time he sets out to find her. In Munich he sees the doll replica of himself in a shop window. It is sold before he can make up his mind to buy it. The doll turns up later depicted in an avant-garde still life of sunflowers and a poached egg. The captain buys the picture and later in agreement with Hannele destroys it. Having found the countess, he pursues a difficult courtship before she accepts him on *his* terms.

It is those terms that are the point of the story. Having been married to a woman who demanded adoration, who reduced him to a puppet, he has no intention of repeating that experience. As he puts it to Hannele: "If a woman loves you, she'll make a doll out of you." He does not want marriage on a basis of love; he wants to be honored and obeyed. "If a woman honours me—absolutely from the bottom of her nature honours me—and obeys me because of that, I take it, my desire for her goes very much deeper than if I was in love with her, or if I adored her." Hannele thinks this subjection a deadly fate for any woman. He counters that on the contrary it is woman's highest fate: "To be a wife—and to be loved and shielded as a wife—not as a flirting woman."

Infelicity in marriage is in *St. Mawr* secondary to general dissatisfaction with contemporary life, almost as an inescapable corollary of the condition. Louise Witt, an American girl, is married to an Australian, Sir Henry Carrington—Rico—a fashionable painter and ornament of society. Between them there is nervous tension rather than spontaneity of passion, with the result that their marriage is soon one without sex. Lou develops increasing contempt for her husband's inner softness and vacuous enjoyments. In contrast to him and the "clipped, shorn, mincing young Englishmen" of her acquaintance is the handsome bay stallion, St. Mawr, which she buys for her husband to ride. The horse is apparently the incarnation of meanness. Though raised for stud, he has so far refused to perform. Lou responds to his maleness. She feels hot life come through to her. Mrs. Witt, her mother, says she has seen no man to compare with St. Mawr. Rico is afraid of him, expecially after he is requested not to ride in Rotten Row anymore because he can't control the stallion. Lou loves St. Mawr because he is not intimate, because he keeps his distance and maintains his integrity. She wishes that human beings might get their lives from the same source as the animals and still be themselves. She sees the god Pan in St. Mawr. Her mother hastens to make a distinction between the unfallen Pan and the hidden Pan, that is, between primal sexual force and a debased, uncreative sexuality.

A further dimension of contrast occurs in the two grooms of the Witt-Carrington establishment.

The Mexican-Navajo, Phoenix, whom Mrs. Witt has brought from America, has a kind of imperviousness and self-sufficiency. The same thing is true of Lewis, the Welsh groom who comes with St. Mawr. Though servants, both men are so impressive by their wholeness that Mrs. Witt thinks of marrying Lewis, and Lou's thoughts stray to the point of recognizing the unsuitability of Phoenix as a husband because of his conception of marriage. Both the grooms accompany Lou and her mother to America after St. Mawr turns on Rico and causes him to break his leg. Lou spirits the horse away before public opinion forces his gelding or destruction. When the time comes, the choice is easy. Lou opts for St. Mawr and America, leaving Rico, who does not need emasculating, to fare as best he can.

Regrettably, the later part of the story is weakened by too much commentary, especially since the general symbolic value of St. Mawr needs no further comment. Once in the Southwest he recovers the will to procreation, and Lou, having found an isolated ranch, seeks a new avatar of contemplation, in which she can "escape from the friction which is the whole stimulus in modern social life." In her mountain retreat "The landscape lived, and lived as the world of the Gods, unsullied and unconcerned. Man did not exist for it." Lou's reflections about "the mysterious potency of evil everywhere" merge with the voice of the narrator, who makes a wide survey of the contemporary situation. He repudiates Bolshevism and Fascism as sources of regeneration. Man has accumulated so much trivia that he must destroy as he goes if a viable society is to emerge. St. Mawr's bad behavior was due to "the slavish malevolence of a domesticated creature." It would have been his fulfillment to serve the brave, reckless, noble men of the past.

The ending is, as usual, indeterminate. Mrs.

Witt is numb in the United States, as she is everywhere, though highly articulate about it. The groom
Lewis resists marriage because women try to "make
you give in to them, so that they feel almighty, and
you feel small." Phoenix has returned to his full being in the Southwest, but Lou now sees his inadequacy clearly: "the aboriginal phallic male in him
simply couldn't recognize her as a woman at all."
She wonders if down deep he is really very different from discarded Rico. The cowboys whom she
meets at a Texas ranch are also vacuous and unreal,
as self-conscious as movie heroes. This disdain on
Lou's part is not necessarily a denial of the primacy
of sex. It is a recognition of the impossibility of it in
the debased modern world.

In all three of these novellas the statement is
strengthened by the presence of a floating symbol,
or symbolic referent—fox, doll, and stallion, respec-
tively. Lawrence's technique here is, as in the
novels, different from that of other writers. His symbols are suggestive, stimulative, without being attached to a rigid and consistent pattern. They serve
to heighten our awareness of a significant characteristic or situation by what is, on occasion, almost an
awkward intrusion on the narrative. They do not develop or accumulate meaning; whenever they appear they merely reenforce the impression they
have already made. And they are dispensable.
When Lawrence is through with them they may
float away, like St. Mawr. In fact, this is preferable to
the arbitrary disposal of them that comes with the
fox and the captain's doll. What Lawrence achieved
by this rather casual technique is a reenforcement
of meaning without being subjected to the artifice
of a tight and articulated image pattern.

8

The Permanence
of Lawrence

Throughout the preceding discussion of Lawrence's prose fiction there has been an uneasy recognition that, great as some of these works are, they are imperfect artifacts. All too often the voice of the author takes over from the removed, objective narrator, arguing instead of showing—which is the proper way of fiction—producing in the reader the same kind of irritation as that which comes from Tolstoy's arguments about determinism in *War and Peace*. Most of the novels could have been written more economically; their labyrinthine repetitions are boring to some readers. More specifically, *Sons and Lovers* suffers from uncertain point of view and distancing. *The Rainbow* is out of scale. *Women in Love* is unnecessarily discursive, though I find it the best balanced of the novels. *Lady Chatterley's Lover* is, self-evidently, as much tract as novel. *The Plumed Serpent*, for all its power, demands acceptance of childish assumptions that are not easy to swallow. The clean lines of *St. Mawr* are broken by insistence on a thesis that the narrative is quite capable of carrying by itself. *The Fox*, most nearly perfect of all, is flawed by the contrived death of Banford. In all these works the symbolic overlay is loosely, even erratically, attached. Yet in the final analysis such flaws and weaknesses do not greatly diminish the impact of these works. What they have to say comes through to those who, following Lawrence's admonition, trust the tale. They live, and willy-nilly the reader lives in and through them.

To Lawrence, formula, or conscientious pursuit of formal structure, is the kiss of death. In his view, "The business of art is to reveal the relation between man and his circumambient universe, *at the living moment*" (italics mine). The novel is actually a process of knowing, a pushing through to a new level of understanding, even to a new consciousness. It must "tackle new propositions without using abstractions; it's got to present us with new, really new feelings, a whole line of new emotion, which will get us out of the emotional rut."

He considers the novel to be "the highest form of human expression so far attained" because it does not set up absolutes. "In a novel, everything is relative to everything else, if that novel is art at all. There may be didactic bits, but they aren't the novel." There is a problem of conflict between a novelist's purpose—that is, his philosophy—and his passional inspiration, but the novel "won't *let* you tell didactic lies, and put them over." It is important to "hear what the novel says. As for the novelist, he is usually a dribbling liar."[1] What Lawrence is saying here is that many novels, like the works of classic American literature which he analyzed, seem to adhere to a tame and conventional view of human behavior, while their passional inspiration is one of phallic worship.

Before examining the body of ideas of which such phallic consciousness is a part, it is worthwhile to look at Lawrence's opinions of other novelists. He scoffs at such popular works as *The Green Hat* and *The Constant Nymph*. He objects that

Arnold Bennett's *Anna of the Five Towns* "seems like an acceptance—so does all the modern stuff since Flaubert. I hate it. I want to wash again quickly, wash off England, the oldness and grubbiness and despair."[2] He takes an equally unfavorable view of Galsworthy's *The Forsyte Saga*, which he considers a missed opportunity for really probing satire. He sometimes wonders if underneath "his rainbow sentimentalism" Galsworthy is not being cynical and rancorous.[3] The three greatest novelists of the twentieth century Lawrence writes off almost completely. Proust is "too much water-jelly—I can't read him."[4] He pays little attention to Joyce except to condemn the last part of *Ulysses* for its dirtiness.[5] Thomas Mann—he apparently knew only the earlier works up to *Royal Highness*—he considers "the last sick sufferer from the complaint of Flaubert. The latter stood away from life as from a leprosy."[6]

The basis of these antagonisms becomes clear in a comment that Byron, Baudelaire, Wilde, and Proust "all did the same thing, or tried to: to kick off, or to intellectualise and so utterly falsify the phallic consciousness, which is the basic consciousness, and the thing we mean, in the best sense, by common sense."[7] On the other hand, greatness in the novel consists in part of doing what Hardy, along with other great writers like Shakespeare, Sophocles, and Tolstoy, did: "setting behind the small action of his protagonists the terrific action of unfathomed nature; setting a smaller system of morality, the one grasped and formulated by the human consciousness, within the vast, uncomprehended and incomprehensible morality of nature or of life itself, surpassing human consciousness." It is noteworthy that Lawrence does not allow Dostoevsky place on this Parnassus. His novels are

great parables and false art. Dostoevsky is "foul" for
mixing God and Sadism.[8]

Lawrence's attitude toward his major realist-
naturalist predecessors is informative. He admired
Zola and did not resent having his own early novels
compared to Zola's works.[9] Possibly he overlooked
Zola's pessimistic determinism in favor of his overwhelming vitality. In the introduction to his transla-
tion of Verga's *Mastro-don Gesualdo*, Lawrence
makes clear what his feelings about realism are:
"The trouble with realism—and Verga was a realist—is that the writer . . . tries to read his own sense
of tragedy into people much smaller than himself."[10] Nonetheless Verga's *Mastro-don Gesualdo*
is "one of the great novels of Europe" because its
hero is "the last forlorn remnant of the Greeks,
blindly but brightly seeking for splendour and self-
enhancement, instead of salvation." His approval
rests in part on the fact that Verga "turned to the
peasants to find, *in individuals*, the vivid spontaneity of sensitive passionate life, non-moral and
non-didactic." Yet, Lawrence has to admit, he found
it "always defeated." He is quick to insist that realism "has no more to do with reality than romanticism has. Realism is just one of the arbitrary views
man takes of man. It sees us all as little ant-like crea-
tures toiling against the odds of circumstance, and
doomed to misery."[11] This is a view to which Lawrence refuses to subscribe.

From these remarks on the novel three major
Lawrence ideas emerge. First is that the novel, and
the poem, are instruments of knowledge. They demand of the writer that he be true to the flame that
is in him. If he is true, then he will, to some extent
at least, be able to define and understand that inner
flame. Second is the primacy of "phallic consciousness," "blood consciousness," or whatever one

wishes to call the wellsprings of action and being beneath analytical rationality. And third is a refusal to accept a doctrine of limits that is central to the pessimistic determinism of the realist in literature and of the behaviorist in psychology.

When we look at these ideas as a body, we realize that Lawrence is in important respects at one with the grand romantics of the nineteenth century—though, in the happy phrase of Lady Cynthia Asquith, "a mystical materialist."[12] Without pushing his affiliation with the English romantic poets too far, we can see that he is Wordsworthian in his feeling for nature and his hatred for the industrial world that mechanizes man. He is Shelleyan in his insistence on sexual union that is almost mystical, Shelleyan too in his feeling that poets should be the legislators of mankind. Without believing in an idealist metaphysics of the Absolute toward union with which the individual should strive, he does take a somewhat comparable materialist position that the individual should strive for being and growth in harmony with the deep-seated passional elements in his nature, a source that is warm and flowing, not chilled and made rigid by reason.

As early as 1913 Lawrence was writing to Ernest Collings that "My great religion is a belief in the blood, the flesh as being wiser than the intellect. We can go wrong in our minds. But what our blood feels and believes and says, is always true. The intellect is only a bit and a bridle. What do I care about knowledge? All I want is to answer my blood, direct, without fribbling intervention of mind, or moral, or what-not. I conceive a man's body as a kind of flame, like a candle flame, forever upright and yet flowing: and the intellect is just the light that is shed onto the things around."[13] A few years later he found himself completely at loggerheads with Bertrand Russell and the Cambridge set to which the mathematician-philosopher belonged. Russell later commented that he had disliked Lawrence's "philosophy of blood," writing "I do not think in retrospect that they [Lawrence's ideas] had any merit whatever. They were the ideas of a sensitive would-be despot who got angry with the world because it would not instantly obey."[14]

In the novels it is the men and women who depend on rational systems who are the failures. Miriam in *Sons and Lovers* refuses to listen to her blood but instead is dominated by divine imperatives. In *The Rainbow* Will Brangwen is shackled by a belief in the Absolute, though it is Anton Skrebensky in his utter unquestioning conformity to the system who is the outstanding failure. Gerald Crich in *Women in Love* is the slave of another kind of conformity, to the industrial machine and the values of an industrial society that not only ignore but dry up the demands of the blood. In *The Plumed Serpent* a whole society suffers from the imposition of alien values, by church and by foreign exploiters, and has to go back to its primitive springs of nonrational being to be restored to life.

It is not sufficiently remarked that Lawrence's belief in the possibility of regeneration, so passionately held, is only inconclusively borne out by his novels. For the most part they end in hope, not in emphatic affirmation. We can, I think, take both *The Lost Girl* and *Lady Chatterley* as positive in statement, though hedged with uncertainties *external* to the protagonists. In general it is to the credit of Lawrence's honesty as chronicler of the human condition that he permits no easy solutions, that he does not let didactic intention triumph over observed limitation, however much he insists that limitation is not an ineluctable barrier.

The goal for Lawrence is not a stasis, not an ultimate condition of beatitude, but process, an effort of the will fueled and directed by underlying passion toward fullness of being. Just as subsidence into a state of mechanical acceptance is anathema to Lawrence, the passivity of Buddha or the gormless meekness of Christ is unacceptable. Nirvana is not for him. As he wrote his friends the Brewsters, "the goal is not that men should become serene as Buddha or as gods, but that the unfleshed gods should become men in battle. God made man is the goal."[15] This idea is expressed vividly in *Etruscan Places*, where his imagination endows that ancient and unknown people with godlike attributes. In primitive days, he says, "The active religious idea was that man, by vivid attention and subtlety and exerting all his strength, could draw more life into himself, more life, more and more glistening vitality, till he became shining like the morning, blazing like a god."

Thus, like many of the romantics, Lawrence does idealize man in a state of nature, primitive nature, and dreams of a return to a preexisting golden age. In his travels he is likely to find, initially, such natural men—in rural Italy, in Sicily, in Sardinia, and further afield in the American Southwest and in Mexico. These expectations do not hold up against observed actuality. It may be that people in these places are more attuned to the basic forces of life, are more natural and more manly, but he never holds them up as shining examples for long. As we have seen in *Lady Chatterley*, he also dreams of a preindustrial England, where men take joy in song and dance, as artists fashion the few things they need, and blazon their soul's well-being by wearing scarlet trousers—in detail as well as spirit pretty much a plagiarism of William Morris, who preceded

him in the quest. The dream of a golden age, of an
Eden before the Fall dies hard. Yet I do not think
Lawrence held to it seriously in his later years.

Like the romantics before him, he also dreamed
of establishing a new freer and more truly humane
society—not on the banks of the Susquehanna, but
perhaps in America, perhaps definitely in New
Mexico, after he had left there. He called this ideal
gathering together of like-minded people Rananim.
The members were to be whomever he was close to
at the time of his active proselytizing, Middleton
Murry and Katherine Mansfield and others during
the war years, Dorothy Brett, Murry and others on
his return from New Mexico, always his friend S. S.
Koteliansky, a Russian refugee and man of letters—
with whom he never quarreled, possibly because
they did not see each other often.

The main thing about Rananim was that it was
to be a refuge from and repudiation of the decay that
Lawrence discerned all about him in England. That
decay is one of his most persistent themes. We find
it in all the later novels and many of the shorter
works of fiction. Its outward sign is ugliness, a destruction of the natural beauty of England by industrialization. He sweepingly wished to clear the
whole mess away: "If only there were not more than
one hundred people in Great Britain!—all the rest
clear space, grass and trees and stone!" In "Nottingham and the Mining Countryside" he asserts that
"The real tragedy of England, as I see it, is the tragedy of ugliness. The country is so lovely: the man-
made England is so vile." In the nineteenth century
"It was ugliness which really betrayed the spirit of
man," condemning the workers to "meanness and
formless and ugly surroundings, ugly ideals, ugly
religion, ugly hope, ugly love, ugly clothes, ugly
furniture, ugly houses, ugly relationship between

workers and employers. The human soul needs actual beauty even more than bread." On a return to
Eastwood late in life, he sounds the same note:
"Wherever you go, there is the sordid sense of humanity"—too many cars, too many people, too
much ugliness. In still another context, he writes of
"the inner tragedy of the English," cut off from the
flow of life, cut off from touch, from living contact.
After the war, eager to get away from Europe as
well as England, he writes of the old civilization as
"a dead dog which begins to stink intolerably," "a
dead dog that died of a love disease like syphilis."

Yet in spite of his denunciation of the fallen
state of his countrymen, as a good romantic he holds
fast to a basic tenet of the romantic point of view, a
belief in the essential goodness of man. That is, he
holds to it most of the time—when he is not hyper-
bolically cutting himself off from the whole human
race because he hates "being squashed into humanity, like a strawberry boiled with all the other straw-
berries into jam." Fundamentally, however, he is
"convinced that the majority of people today have
good, generous feelings which they can never
know, never experience, because of some fear,
some repression. I do not believe that people would
be villains, thieves, murderers and sexual criminals
if they were freed from legal restraints . . . I am convinced that people want to be more decent, more
good-hearted than our social system of money and
grab allows them to be . . ." This statement ties in
directly with Lawrence's dreams of Rananim,
which was to be "a community established on the
assumption of goodness in its members, instead of
the assumption of badness."

By his repudiation of current attitudes and us-
ages Lawrence was a true radical. As Herbert Asquith commented, though far removed "from the

dust of politics," he was "more deeply in revolt
against the values of the age than any political
leader."[16] Moreover, Lawrence had no use for the
nostrums of party or social movement: "I am convinced, if one is to do anything real in this Country,
one must eschew all connection with Fabianism,
Socialism, Cambridgeism, and advancedism of all
sorts, like poison . . . One must go out on one's own,
unadhering."[17] As we have seen, this attitude is
echoed in *Kangaroo*, the most political of the
novels. Though Lawrence toys with the problem of
leadership in *Aaron's Rod*, *Kangaroo*, and *The
Plumed Serpent*, he does not really offer any solution to that problem. Radical renovation must come,
but it must come from within. In spite of the charge
that his views would lead to fascism he was scornful
of the Mussolini regime in Italy and would, I think,
have seen through the blood-brotherhood trappings
of Nazism in Germany.

The way to radical renovation from within is
blood consciousness, as Lawrence repeatedly and
insistently proclaims. In his foreword to *Women in
Love* he sums up what he had long been saying:
"Let us hesitate no longer to announce that the sensual passions and mysteries are equally sacred with
the spiritual mysteries and passions. Who would
deny it any more? The only thing unbearable is the
degradation, the prostitution of the living mysteries
in us. Let man only approach his own self with a
deep respect, even reverence for all that the creative soul, the God-mystery within us puts forth . . .
Nothing that comes from the deep, passional soul is
bad, or can be bad." At the end of his life, in "Introduction to these Paintings," he expresses the idea
more combatively: "The history of our era is the
nauseating and repulsive history of the crucifixion
of the procreative body for the glorification of the

spirit, the mental consciousness. Plato was the arch-
priest of this crucifixion." In "The State of Funk" he
advises his readers to get out of their state of sex
funk, that is, cowardice. To do so they must accept
sex fully in the consciousness: "Accept the sexual,
physical being of yourself, and of every other creature. Don't be afraid of it. Don't be afraid of the
physical functions. Don't be afraid of the so-called
obscene words . . . Conquer the fear of sex and re-
store the natural flow [of human sympathy]."

Lawrence puts the blame for the divided self
on Christianity and other doctrines that emphasize
the soul at the expense of the body, though he does
note with approval that the Catholic church in
southern countries makes marriage a sacrament
based on sexual communion. This is right because
"The man is a potential creator, and in this lies his
splendour." Historically in Europe it was during the
Renaissance that fear of sex developed. By one of
his wildest flights of speculation he blames this on
the shock of syphilis, which appeared about that
time. He finds that "physical consciousness gives a
last song in Burns, then is dead." After that point in
literature as in life, "The essential instinctive-intui-
tive body is dead, and worshipped in death—all
very unhealthy."

Any regeneration of society must be based on
individual regeneration, or rather on the nucleus
that is provided by a sexually healthy marriage,
without which there can be neither wholeness nor
harmony. It is not necessary to retrace the steps we
have taken through the novels and shorter fictions
in examination of various states of sexual ill-being
or well-being. What is important is to try to determine, from the exhibits provided, what that marital
well-being is. Lawrence tries to describe a state in
which the partners are both fused in passional

union and yet retain their individuality, in other
words are separate yet equal. Somehow, though,
that equality for women looks remarkably like sub-
ordination to a supporting role. There is a good deal
of warrant for considering Lawrence a male chau-
vinist.

If we recall for a moment the formula offered
by Alexander Hepburn in *The Captain's Doll*, "To
be a wife—and to be loved and shielded as a wife,"
we can see that while a woman has a role beyond
that of sex object, it is inconceivable that she should
be the dominant member of the conjugal partner-
ship. I think it is clear that Lawrence has sympathy
for women and interest in their development—up
to a point. To take the three prime examples, Ursula
Brangwen, Alvina Houghton, and Constance Chatterley, their self-enfranchisement is a matter of moment in which the reader is led to rejoice. But in
each case what they are freeing themselves from is
meaningless convention and spinsterhood or sterile
marriage. It is pretty certain in all three cases that it
is the male partner who will call the tune. The
values of loyalty, of quiet submissiveness, of emotional balance against the vagaries of the male cannot be overprized, but the fact remains that there is
no place in Lawrence's world for the woman who
strikes out on her own or for the male who is content to take a secondary place in the union.

What I have been saying with gentle circum-
spection is that Lawrence's ideas are not particularly original or particularly arresting. They are off-
shoots of his effort at self-discovery, not to be
codified as tablets of the law. A sensitive being in
conflict with the values and institutions of the first
quarter of the twentieth century, he emits sparks as
he encounters the resistance of adamantine atti-

tudes and customs. These expository sparks illumi-
nate for a moment, they no doubt do cast some light
on the novels and stories, but we could do without
such explanation without diminishing the impact of
those works. Analytical reasoning is not Lawrence's
forte, and there is no reason to assail him for that
lack.

And so we come back to the novels and short
stories as the basis of Lawrence's power and influence. His works are remarkably undated after more
than sixty years. This is because he is little concerned about outward forms; in only the broadest
terms can he be called a social chronicler. His attention is on those conditions that diminish, even atro-
phy, the living human being: deterioration of the
natural environment; reduction of the individual to
robot, to adjunct of the machine; and spiritual impotence arising from stifled or misdirected sexuality.
All these conditions have worsened in the years
since his death. Physical health as well as aesthetic
joy are imperiled by the environment. Work is increasingly divorced from personal satisfaction. So
much energy is devoted to making a living that actual living, after working hours, becomes passive,
inert, before the television set or as spectator in the
colosseum. The sexual revolution, of which Lawrence is popularly reputed to be one of the principal
leaders, has swept away all barriers. It has produced
a sexual freedom as joyless, mechanical, and unre-
verential as the condition against which he in-
veighed.

In short, the crushing materialist determinism
of the modern age goes on unabated. Whether it is
possible to escape it is ultimately unimportant. We
need to think that we can. It is Lawrence who with
incomparable vigor and honesty attempted to show

the way out, in terms not of transcendental union with a remote Absolute but in terms of innate, instinctual powers belonging to the material man and woman. Among men of letters he has made the most believably affirmative statement since Tolstoy. His novels and stories will continue to be read.

Notes

Epigraph

From a letter to Frieda Lawrence Ravagli, E. W. Tedlock, Jr. (ed.), *Frieda Lawrence: The Memoirs and Correspondence* (New York: Knopf, 1964), p. 401.

1. Fugitive and Seeker

1. Ford Madox Ford, *Portraits from Life* (Boston: Houghton, 1937), pp. 80–81. See also Edward Nehls (ed.), *D. H. Lawrence: A Composite Biography* (Madison: University of Wisconsin Press, 1957–1959), 1: 115.*
2. Aldous Huxley (ed.), *Letters of D. H. Lawrence* (New York: Viking, 1932), p. xxx.
3. David Garnett, *The Golden Echo* (New York: Harcourt, 1954), p. 241. *CB* I: 173.
4. Cecil Gray, *Musical Chairs* (London: Home & Van Thal, 1948). *CB* I: 418.
5. Rachel Annand Taylor in a letter to Richard Aldington, quoted in his *Portrait of an Artist But . . .* (New York: Duell, Sloan & Pearce, 1950), p. 109. *CB* I: 137.

---

*Wherever possible reference is made to the *Composite Biography* (*CB*) as the source most readily accessible to readers.

6. Edmund Wilson, *The Twenties* (New York: Farrar, Straus and Giroux, 1975), p. 149.

7. Ford, *op. cit.*, p. 82. *CB* I: 116.

8. Catherine Carswell, *The Savage Pilgrimage: A Narrative of D. H. Lawrence* (London: Martin Secker, 1932), pp. 66–69. *CB* I: 393.

9. Witter Bynner, *Journey with Genius* (New York: John Day, 1951), pp. 68–69. *CB* II: 220.

10. John Middleton Murry, *Between Two Worlds* (New York: Julian Messner, 1936), p. 333. *CB* I: 277.

11. Gray, *op. cit.*, p. 137. *CB* I: 436.

12. Giuseppe Orioli, *Adventures of a Bookseller* (New York: McBride, 1932), pp. 23–24. *CB* III: 187.

13. Cecil Gray, *Peter Warlock* (London: Jonathan Cape, 1938), p. 114. *CB* I: 348.

14. In a letter dated December 9, 1951, E. W. Tedlock, Jr. (ed.), *Frieda Lawrence: The Memoirs and Correspondence* (New York: Knopf, 1964), p. 340.

15. In a letter dated January 14, 1955, *ibid.*, p. 390.

16. In a letter dated August 29, 1953, *ibid.*, p. 361.

17. In a letter dated December 19, 1951, *ibid.*, p. 341.

18. In a letter dated November 25, 1951, *ibid.*, p. 338.

19. In a letter dated May 22, 1956, *ibid.*, p. 412.

20. Bertrand Russell, "Portraits from Memory—III: D. H. Lawrence," *Harper's Magazine* 206 (February 1953): 93–95. *CB* I: 285.

21. Richard Aldington, *Life for Life's Sake* (New York: Viking, 1941), p. 234. *CB* I: 508.

22. Quoted in Knud Merrild, *A Poet and Two Painters: A Memoir of D. H. Lawrence* (New York: Viking, 1939). *CB* II: 210.

23. Harriet Monroe, *Poetry* 34 (May 1930): 92–94. *CB* II: 330.

24. Carswell, *op. cit.*, pp. 17–21. *CB* I: 228.

25. Huxley, *op. cit.*, p. xxix. *CB* I: 207.

26. *CB* III: 70.

27. Rhys Davies, *Horizon* 2 (October 1940): 207. *CB* III: 316.

28. Huxley, *op. cit.*, pp. xxviii–xxix. *CB* I: 340.

29. From a letter by Heseltine to Frederick Delius

dated April 22, 1916, Gray, *Peter Warlock. CB* I: 351.

30. Bynner, *op. cit.,* pp. 136–137. *CB* II: 233.
31. A letter to the editor of *Composite Biography* dated February 9, 1954, *CB* I: 306.
32. Frieda Lawrence, *"Not I, But the Wind ..."* (New York: Viking, 1934), p. 41. *CB* I: 171.
33. Sandra M. Gilbert, *Acts of Attention: The Poems of D. H. Lawrence* (Ithaca, N.Y.: Cornell University Press, 1972), pp. 92–93.
34. *Ibid.,* p. 132.
35. W. H. Auden, "D. H. Lawrence," *The Dyer's Hand and Other Essays* (London: Faber and Faber, 1963), pp. 277–278.
36. *Ibid.,* p. 288.
37. *Ibid.,* p. 291.
38. A letter dated May 28, 1927, in Mabel Dodge Luhan, *Lorenzo in Taos* (New York: Knopf, 1932), p. 330.
39. *Studies in Classic American Literature* (New York: Thomas Seltzer, 1923), p. 93.
40. *Ibid.,* pp. 121–122.
41. *Ibid.,* p. 164.
42. *Ibid.,* p. 238.
43. *Ibid.,* pp. 257 ff.
44. Earl and Achsah Brewster, *D. H. Lawrence: Reminiscences and Correspondence* (London: Martin Secker, 1934), pp. 117–118. *CB* III: 128.
45. Paul Konody, *The Observer* (London), June 16, 1929. *CB* III: 336.

2. *Sons and Lovers*

1. Ivy Low Litvinov, *Harper's Bazaar* (No. 2818, October 1948), pp. 411–418. *CB* I: 215.
2. E. T. (Jessie Chambers), *D. H. Lawrence: A Personal Record* (London: Jonathan Cape, 1935), pp. 202–204. *CB* I: 147–148.
3. Frieda Lawrence, *"Not I, But the Wind ..."* (New York: Viking, 1934), pp. 56–57. *CB* I: 182.

4. Edward Marsh, *A Number of People: A Book of Reminiscences* (New York: Harper, 1939), pp. 227–228. *CB* I: 359.
5. Edward D. McDonald (ed.), *Phoenix: The Posthumous Papers* (London: Heinemann, 1936), p. 233. *CB* I: 145.

3. *The Rainbow*

1. Edward D. McDonald (ed.), *Phoenix: The Posthumous Papers* (London: Heinemann, 1936), p. 234. *CB* I: 328, 332–335.

4. *Women in Love*

1. John Middleton Murry, *Between Two Worlds* (New York: Julian Messner, 1936), pp. 410–417. *CB* I: 377–381.
2. London *Times*, September 17, 1921.

6. *The Lesser Novels*

1. Eliseo Vivas, *D. H. Lawrence: The Failure and the Triumph of Art* (Evanston, Ill.: Northwestern University Press, 1960). Vivas considers all the novels except *Sons and Lovers, The Rainbow,* and *Women in Love* to be failures.
2. Carleton Beals, *Glass Houses: Ten Years of Free-Lancing* (Philadelphia: Lippincott, 1938), pp. 186–189. *CB* II: 227–229.
3. In a letter dated January 19, 1928, *CB* III: 176–177.

8. *The Permanence of Lawrence*

1. "The Novel," Edward D. McDonald (ed.), *Phoenix* (London: Heinemann, 1936), pp. 416–426.

2. In a letter dated October 6, 1912, Anthony Beal (ed.), *Selected Literary Criticism* (New York: Viking, 1956), p. 131.

3. "John Galsworthy," *ibid.,* pp. 118–131.

4. In a letter dated July 1927, *ibid.,* p. 147.

5. *CB* II: 345.

6. Beal, *op. cit.,* p. 265.

7. *Ibid.,* p. 148.

8. John Middleton Murry, *Between Two Worlds* (New York: Julian Messner, 1936), p. 24. *CB* I: 386.

9. *CB* II: 411.

10. McDonald, *op. cit.,* p. 226.

11. Warren Roberts and Harry T. Moore (eds.), *Phoenix II* (New York: Viking, 1968), p. 281.

12. Cynthia Asquith, *Remember and Be Glad* (London: James Barrie, 1952), pp. 142–144. *CB* I: 443.

13. In a letter dated January 17, 1913, James T. Boulton (ed.), *The Letters of D. H. Lawrence* (Cambridge: Cambridge University Press, 1979), I: 503.

14. Bertrand Russell, *Harper's Magazine* 206 (February 1953): 93–95. *CB* I: 284–285.

15. In a letter dated January 2, 1922, *CB* II: 103.

16. Herbert Asquith, *Moments of Memory: Recollections and Impressions* (New York: Scribners, 1938), p. 182. *CB* I: 201.

17. In a letter to Barbara Low dated December 11, 1916, *CB* I: 407.

Bibliography

Books by D. H. Lawrence

The White Peacock, New York: Duffield, 1911; London: Heinemann, 1911.

The Trespasser, London: Duckworth, 1912; New York: Mitchell Kennerley, 1912.

Love Poems and Others, London: Duckworth, 1913; New York: Mitchell Kennerley, 1913.

Sons and Lovers, London: Duckworth, 1913; New York: Mitchell Kennerley, 1913.

The Widowing of Mrs. Holroyd, London: Duckworth, 1914; New York: Mitchell Kennerley, 1914.

The Prussian Officer and Other Stories, London: Duckworth, 1914; New York: B. W. Huebsch, 1916.

The Rainbow, London: Methuen, 1915; New York: B. W. Huebsch, 1916 (expurgated text).

Amores, London: Duckworth, 1916; New York: B. W. Huebsch, 1916.

Twilight in Italy, London: Duckworth, 1916; New York: B. W. Huebsch, 1916.

Look! We Have Come Through!, London: Chatto, 1917; New York: B. W. Huebsch, 1918.

New Poems, London: Martin Secker, 1918; New York: B. W. Huebsch, 1920.

Touch and Go, London: C. W. Daniel, 1920; New York: Thomas Seltzer, 1920.

The Lost Girl, London: Martin Secker, 1920; New York: Thomas Seltzer, 1921.

Women in Love, London: Martin Secker, 1921; New York:
   Thomas Seltzer, 1922.

Movements in European History, London: Oxford University Press, 1921, under the pseudonym of Lawrence H. Davison.

Psychoanalysis and the Unconscious, New York: Thomas
   Seltzer, 1921; London: Martin Secker, 1923.

Sea and Sardinia, New York: Thomas Seltzer, 1921; London: Martin Secker, 1923.

Aaron's Rod, New York: Thomas Seltzer, 1922; London:
   Martin Secker, 1922.

England, My England and Other Stories, New York: Thomas Seltzer, 1922; London: Martin Secker, 1924.

Fantasia of the Unconscious, New York: Thomas Seltzer,
   1922; London: Martin Secker, 1923.

The Captain's Doll, New York: Thomas Seltzer, 1923;
   London: Martin Secker, 1923, with the title: *The Ladybird*.

Studies in Classic American Literature, New York: Thomas Seltzer, 1923; London: Martin Secker, 1924.

Kangaroo, New York: Thomas Seltzer, 1923; London:
   Martin Secker, 1923.

Birds, Beasts and Flowers, New York: Thomas Seltzer,
   1923; London: Martin Secker, 1923.

St. Mawr: Together with The Princess, London: Martin
   Secker, 1925; New York: Knopf, 1925, with title *St.
   Mawr*.

*Reflections on the Death of a Porcupine and Other Es-
   says*, Philadelphia: Centaur Press, 1925; London:
   Martin Secker, 1934.

The Plumed Serpent (Quetzalcoatl), New York: Knopf,
   1926; London: Martin Secker, 1926.

David, London: Martin Secker, 1926; New York: Knopf,
   1926.

Mornings in Mexico, New York: Knopf, 1927; London:
   Martin Secker, 1927.

The Woman Who Rode Away and Other Stories, New
   York: Knopf, 1928; London: Martin Secker, 1928.

Lady Chatterley's Lover, Florence: privately printed,

1928; Paris: privately printed, 1929; New York: Knopf, 1932 (Authorized Abridged Edition); London: Martin Secker, 1932 (Authorized Abridged Edition); New York: Grove Press, 1959 (unexpurgated edition); London: Penguin, 1961 (unexpurgated edition).

Collected Poems, in two volumes, New York: Jonathan Cape and Harrison Smith, 1928; London: Martin Secker, 1928.

Pansies, London: Martin Secker, 1929; New York: Knopf, 1929.

Pornography and Obscenity, New York: Knopf, 1930.

Assorted Articles, New York: Knopf, 1930.

A Propos of Lady Chatterley's Lover, London: Mandrake Press, 1930, Heinemann, 1931.

Love among the Haystacks and Other Pieces, London: Nonesuch Press, 1930; New York: Viking, 1933.

The Man Who Died, London: Martin Secker, 1931; New York: Knopf, 1931. First published under the title, *The Escaped Cock,* Paris: Black Sun Press, 1929.

Etruscan Places, New York: Viking, 1932; London: Martin Secker, 1932.

Last Poems, Florence: G. Orioli, 1932; New York: Viking, 1933; London: Heinemann, 1935.

The Lovely Lady and Other Stories, New York: Viking, 1933; London: Martin Secker, 1933.

The Plays of D. H. Lawrence, London: Martin Secker, 1933.

A Modern Lover, New York: Viking, 1934; London: Martin Secker, 1934.

Phoenix: The Posthumous Papers of D. H. Lawrence, edited by Edward D. McDonald, New York: Viking, 1936.

The First Lady Chatterley, New York: Dial Press, 1944.

Phoenix II: Uncollected, Unpublished, and Other Prose Works by D. H. Lawrence, edited by Warren Roberts and Harry T. Moore, New York: Viking, 1968.

John Thomas and Lady Jane (the second *Lady Chatterley*), New York: Viking, 1972.

The Letters of D. H. Lawrence, edited by James T.

Boulton, Cambridge: Cambridge University Press, vol. I (September 1901–May 1903), 1979. This complete edition will appear in eight volumes.

Books about D. H. Lawrence

Aldington, Richard, *D. H. Lawrence: Portrait of a Genius But . . .* , New York: Duell, Sloan and Pearce, 1950.

Alldritt, Keith, *Visual Imagination of D. H. Lawrence*, London: Edward Arnold, 1971.

Auden, W. H., *The Dyer's Hand and Other Essays*, London: Faber and Faber, 1968; "D. H. Lawrence," pp. 277–295.

Brett, Dorothy, *Lawrence and Brett: A Friendship*, Philadelphia: Lippincott, 1933.

Brewster, Earl H. and Achsah, *D. H. Lawrence: Reminiscences and Correspondence*, London: Martin Secker, 1934.

Bynner, Witter, *Journey with Genius: Recollections and Reflections Concerning the D. H. Lawrences*, New York: Day, 1951.

Callow, Philip, *Son and Lover: The Young D. H. Lawrence*, New York: Stein and Day, 1975.

Carswell, Catherine, *The Savage Pilgrimage: A Narrative of D. H. Lawrence*, London: Martin Secker, 1932.

Carter, Frederick, *D. H. Lawrence and the Body Mystical*, London: Denis Archer, 1932.

Cavitch, David, *D. H. Lawrence and the New World*, New York: Oxford University Press, 1969.

Clarke, Colin C., *River of Dissolution*, London: Routledge & K. Paul, 1969.

Corke, Helen, *D. H. Lawrence: The Croydon Years*, Austin: University of Texas Press, 1965.

Cowan, James C., *D. H. Lawrence's American Journey*, Cleveland: Case Western Reserve University Press, 1970.

Daleski, Herman N., *The Forked Flame*, Evanston, Ill.: Northwestern University Press, 1965.

Davies, Rhys, "D. H. Lawrence in Bandol," *Horizon* 2 (No. 10, October 1940), 191–208.

Delany, Paul, *D. H. Lawrence's Nightmare: The Writer and His Circle in the Years of the Great War,* New York: Basic Books, 1978.

Delavenay, Emile, *D. H. Lawrence: The Man and His Work. The Formative Years: 1885–1919,* London: Heinemann, 1972.

Draper, Ronald P., *D. H. Lawrence: The Critical Heritage,* New York: Barnes & Noble, 1970.

Fay, Eliot G., *Lorenzo in Search of the Sun,* New York: Bookman, 1953.

Ford, George H., *Double Measure: A Study of the Novels and Stories of D. H. Lawrence,* New York: Holt, Rinehart and Winston, 1965.

Foster, Joseph O., *D. H. Lawrence in Taos,* Albuquerque: University of New Mexico Press, 1972.

Gilbert, Sandra M., *Acts of Attention: The Poems of D. H. Lawrence,* Ithaca, N.Y.: Cornell University Press, 1972.

Gomme, A. H. (ed.), *D. H. Lawrence: A Critical Study of the Major Novels and Other Writings,* New York: Barnes & Noble, 1978.

Goodheart, Eugene, *The Utopian Vision of D. H. Lawrence,* Chicago: University of Chicago Press, 1963.

Gordon, David J., *D. H. Lawrence as a Literary Critic,* New Haven, Conn.: Yale University Press, 1966.

Gregory, Horace, *D. H. Lawrence: Pilgrim of the Apocalypse,* New York: Grove Press, 1957.

Hojman, Baruj, *Another Ego,* Columbia: University of South Carolina Press, 1970.

Howe, Marguerite B., *The Art of Self in D. H. Lawrence,* Athens: Ohio University Press, 1977.

Jarrett-Kerr, William H., *D. H. Lawrence and Human Existence,* London: Rockliff, 1951.

Kermode, Frank, *D. H. Lawrence,* New York: Viking, 1973.

Lawrence, Ada, and G. Stuart Gelder, *Early Life of D. H.*

Lawrence: Together with Hitherto Unpublished Letters and Articles, London: Martin Secker, 1932.

Lawrence, Frieda, *"Not I, But the Wind . . .,"* New York: Viking, 1934.

Leavis, F. R., *D. H. Lawrence, Novelist,* New York: Simon and Schuster, 1955.

———, *Thought, Words and Creativity: Art and Thought in Lawrence,* New York: Oxford University Press, 1976.

Levy, Mervyn (ed.), *Paintings of D. H. Lawrence,* New York: Viking, 1964.

Luhan, Mabel Dodge, *Lorenzo in Taos,* New York: Knopf, 1932.

Marshall, Tom, *The Psychic Mariner: A Reading of the Poems of D. H. Lawrence,* New York: Viking, 1970.

Miko, Stephen J., *Toward Women in Love: The Emergence of a Lawrentian Aesthetic,* New Haven, Conn.: Yale University Press, 1971.

Moore, Harry T., *D. H. Lawrence: The Man and His Works,* Toronto: Forum House, 1969.

———, *The Intelligent Heart,* New York: Farrar, Straus and Young, 1954.

———, *The Priest of Love,* New York: Farrar, Straus and Giroux, 1974.

Moynahan, Julian, *The Deed of Life,* Princeton, N.J.: Princeton University Press, 1963.

Murry, John Middleton, *Reminiscences of D. H. Lawrence,* London: Jonathan Cape, 1933.

Nehls, Edward (ed.), *D. H. Lawrence: A Composite Biography,* in three volumes, Madison: University of Wisconsin Press, 1957, 1958, 1959.

Niven, Alastair, *D. H. Lawrence: The Novels,* New York: Cambridge University Press, 1978.

Pinion, F. B., *A D. H. Lawrence Companion: Life, Thought and Works,* London: Macmillan, 1978.

Pritchard, Ronald E., *D. H. Lawrence: Body of Darkness,* Pittsburgh: University of Pittsburgh Press, 1971.

Sagar, Keith M., *The Art of D. H. Lawrence,* New York: Cambridge University Press, 1966.

————, *D. H. Lawrence: A Calendar of His Works*, Austin: University of Texas Press, 1979.

Sanders, Scott, *D. H. Lawrence: The World of the Five Major Novels*, New York: Viking, 1974.

Slade, Tony, *D. H. Lawrence*, New York: Arco, 1970.

Spender, Stephen, *D. H. Lawrence: Novelist, Poet, Prophet*, New York: Harper & Row, 1973.

Spilka, Mark (ed.), *D. H. Lawrence: A Collection of Critical Essays*, Englewood Cliffs, N.J.: Prentice-Hall, 1964.

————, *The Love Ethic of D. H. Lawrence*, Bloomington: Indiana University Press, 1955.

Swigg, Richard, *Lawrence, Hardy, and American Literature*, New York: Oxford University Press, 1972.

T., E. (Jessie Chambers), *D. H. Lawrence: A Personal Record*, London: Jonathan Cape, 1935.

Tedlock, E. W., *D. H. Lawrence, Artist and Rebel: A Study of Lawrence's Fiction*, Albuquerque: University of New Mexico Press, 1963.

Vivas, Eliseo, *D. H. Lawrence: The Failure and the Triumph of Art*, Evanston, Ill.: Northwestern University Press, 1960.

Widner, Kingsley, *The Art of Perversity: D. H. Lawrence's Shorter Fiction*, Seattle: University of Washington Press, 1962.

Index

MODERN LITERATURE MONOGRAPHS

In the same series: (continued from p. ii)